Skills for writing

Ann Mann
Codsall High School, Staffordshire
Hilary Rich
Chase Terrace High School, Staffordshire

Book 2   an examination course

Longman

Contents

Introduction

Each section of this book deals with a different type of writing.
The skills needed are listed at the beginning of each chapter.
The skills list shows you at a glance what the important areas
are. Use it as a checklist when preparing for an examination.
The extracts have been chosen to give examples of a wide
range of writing styles and to draw your attention to ways in
which writers organise and express their ideas. The full range of
extracts, authors, and sources is on page 147.

From first draft to final copy

To produce your best work, you must be prepared to spend time **planning**, making a **first draft**, and **revising** it. Here are stages from a pupil's work.

The plan

What I can see	What I can hear	What I can smell/taste	What I can feel
Blackness at first small latticed windows sunlight - a ray furniture - chairs, bookcase, dust, cabinet, ornaments pictures on walls hanging curtains threadbare carpet wallpaper- faded and peeling	Silence stillness Later a creaking door Own breathing	mustiness stale air dustiness dirt	dampness claustrophobia

The first draft

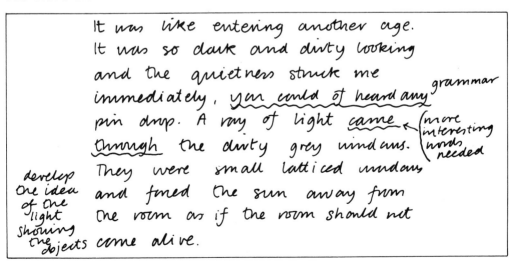

It was like entering another age. It was so dark and dirty looking and the quietness struck me immediately, you could of heard any pin drop. A ray of light came through the dirty grey windows. They were small latticed windows and forced the sun away from the room as if the room should not objects come alive.

grammar

more interesting words needed

develop one idea of the light showing the objects

The furniture was exquisit. The chairs were big and had big mahogany arm-rests. They were covered with a heavy material with big green flowers printed on. A Louis V chair was in the corner of the room, deeply engraved down its thick legs. The curtains hung loosely from the windows over on the other side of the room stood a tall dark bookshelf full of old tattered books. There was dust everywhere and it had been ages since anyone had opened this room up. The intense musty smell was everywhere.

The second draft

It was like entering another age. It was dark, almost tomb-like, and the quietness immediately struck me. You could have heard a pin drop. The small latticed windows were grey with dirt and seemed to force the sun away from the room, as if it should not come to life.

Slowly, a ray of light seeped through the dirt encrusted glass, and showed me something of the room. Curtains hung limply from the windows. There was dust everywhere.

The furniture was exquisite. The chairs were big and hefty with large mahogany arm-rests. They were covered with a heavy material decorated with green flowers. A Louis V chair, deeply engraved down its sturdy legs, sat peacefully in the corner of the room. On the other side of the room, stood a tall dark bookcase, full of old tattered books. Dust lingered everywhere, and an intense musty smell hovered about the room. It had been ages since anyone had opened it up.

Look at the first and final draft carefully. What changes have been made? How successful are they?

This method will help you produce your best pieces of work, which can be collected together to produce a folio of your writing.

1 Narrative writing

A narrative essay is one which tells a story. The story must be interesting. You need to work out the plot of the story. Make a plan before you begin the essay. Get the reader interested from the beginning. Try to keep that interest until the end.

How to begin

Work out what your story is to be about by answering these questions.

Who are the people the story is going to be about?

Where is the story to take place?

When does the story take place? (the time of day; the season of the year; in the past, the present or the future)

What are the details of the plot of the story?

In a narrative essay it is important that the people who are **the main characters** are described straightaway. The **place** where the story is set, the **time**, and the beginnings of the **plot** also need to be made clear in the opening few paragraphs.

Here are the opening paragraphs of two stories. Read them and answer the questions which follow.

Besieged

Hurly stands behind the half-drawn curtain so that he can look into the street, but can't be seen from it. The police have mounted three huge searchlights on tripods, and they light up the ground outside the artificial daylight of a football field. The glare from two of them is directly in Hurly's eyes. The third is out of sight, mounted outside one of the adjoining buildings. If he pushes his head back, right up against the frame of the window, he can see wire barriers that have been thrown up thirty yards down the street. Beyond the encircling barriers, just outside the circle of light, he can sense the presence of an unnumbered crowd. Their audience. Now and again he fancies that the flash of a camera has burst above the heads of those people, but he can't be sure: it may be some other kind of flare.

Within the circle of light nobody moves. At the edge of the circle, just under the window out of which he is looking, Hurly can see a blue uniformed policeman standing casually, his arms behind his back, his head perpetually sideways like the face on a coin. Below his blue starred helmet the clean-cut features are unrecognisable.

from *The Siege of Babylon* by Farrukh Dhondy

Radio Silence

The radio was the first indication that anything was wrong. Right in the middle of Terry Wogan, on a Friday morning, it went dead. No fuss or bother, just silence. Ken gave his 'tranny' a dirty look over the rim of his teacup and hit it with the flat of his hand, but it stayed dead. He took the back off and poked it with a knife, but failed even to raise a crackle of static. Touching the terminals of the battery to his tongue made him see sparks, so it wasn't that. He sat looking at the gutted corpse of his radio and chewed absently on a piece of cold toast. A radio wasn't something he could fix, so it meant a ten-mile ride to the village to get it seen to. Ken looked up at the window, scoured with rain, and frowned, tomorrow maybe.

Outside the rain lashed and drummed the hills. He stood at the window sipping his tea and watching the rain stipple the loch's surface, and scratched meditatively at the beard he was trying to grow.

from *Fool's Gold* by David Hutchinson

1 For both extracts explain what you found out about – the main characters, the places, and time in the stories.
2 Using the clues given in these opening paragraphs, explain what you think the rest of each story will be about.
3 What kind of stories would begin with these introductions?

Planning a story

Planning helps you to organise your ideas.
Read the following story and answer the questions which follow. They will help you learn how to **organise** a story, and write a plan.

Cemetery Path

Ivan was a timid little man – so timid that the villagers called him 'Pigeon' or mocked him with the title 'Ivan the Terrible'. Every night Ivan stopped in at the saloon on the edge of the village cemetery. Ivan never crossed the cemetery to get to his lonely shack on the other side. The path through the cemetery would save him many minutes, but Ivan had never taken it – not even in the full light of the moon.

Late one winter's night, when a bitter wind and snow beat against the village saloon, the customers took up their familiar mockery of Ivan. His mild protests only fed their taunts, and they laughed when a young Cossack lieutenant flung a challenge at their quarry. 'You are a pigeon, Ivan. A rabbit. A coward. You'll walk all around the cemetery in this dreadful cold, to get home, but you dare not cross the cemetery.'

Ivan murmured, 'The cemetery – it is nothing to cross, Lieutenant. I am not afaid. The cemetery is nothing but earth.'

The Lieutenant cried, 'A challenge, then! Cross the cemetery tonight Ivan, now, and I'll give you five gold roubles – five gold roubles!'

Perhaps it was the vodka. Perhaps it was the temptation of the five gold roubles. No one ever knew why Ivan, moistening his lips, blurted: 'All right Lieutenant, I'll cross the cemetery!'

As the saloon echoed with the villagers' derision and disbelief, the Lieutenant winked to the other and unbuckled his sabre. 'Here Ivan. Prove yourself. When you get to the very centre of the cemetery, in front of the biggest tomb, stick my sabre into the ground. In the morning we shall go there. And if the sabre is in the ground – five gold roubles to you!'

Slowly Ivan took the sabre. The villagers drank a toast: 'To Ivan the Hero! Ivan the Terrible!' They roared with laughter.

The wind howled around Ivan as he closed the door of the saloon behind him. The cold was as sharp as a butcher's knife. He buttoned his long coat and crossed the dirt road. He could hear the lieutenant's voice, louder than the rest, calling after him, 'Five roubles, little pigeon! Five roubles – if you live!'

Ivan strode to the cemetery gates, and hesitated, and pushed the gate open.

He walked fast. 'Earth, it's just earth . . . like any other earth.' But the darkness was a massive dread. 'Five gold roubles . . .' The wind was savage, and the sabre was like ice in his hands. Ivan shivered under the long, thick coat and broke into a limping run.

He recognised the large tomb. No one could miss that huge edifice. Ivan must have sobbed – but that was drowned in the wind. And Ivan kneeled, cold and terrified, and in a frenzy of fear drove the sabre into the hard ground. It was hard to do, but he beat it down into the hard earth with his fist, down to the very hilt. It was done! The cemetery . . . the challenge . . . five gold roubles . . . five gold roubles!

Ivan started to rise from his knees. But he could not move. Something was holding him! He strained to rise again. But something gripped him in an unyielding, implacable hold. Ivan swore and tugged and lurched and pulled – gasping in his panic, sweating despite the knife-edged cold, shaken by fear. But something held Ivan. He cried out in terror and strained against the unseen imprisonment, and he tried to rise, using all his strength. But he could not rise.

They found Ivan the next morning, on the ground right in front of the great tomb that was in the very centre of the cemetery. His face was not that of a frozen man, but of a man slain by some nameless horror. And the lieutenant's

sabre was in the ground where Ivan had pounded it –
through the dragging folds of his long and shabby coat.

Leonard Ross

1 Why do the villagers and the Cossack lieutenant tease Ivan about the cemetery?
2 What is the lieutenant's challenge?
3 What does he ask Ivan to do to prove he has carried out the dare?
4 What does Ivan do when he leaves the saloon?
5 What has happened to Ivan in the end?

The plan for *Cemetery Path*

Your answers to the questions give you the main stages of the story. When you write a plan, use these main stages as headings. Use capital letters for them. Then make detailed notes of the other points underneath the headings.

IVAN IS AFRAID TO CROSS THE CEMETERY

Well-known Ivan afraid to go through the cemetery, timid. The path through cemetery quickest way home. Ivan would not go that way even in bright moonlight.

THE LIEUTENANT'S CHALLENGE

Must cross the cemetery. Offered 5 gold roubles. Ivan tempted by money, or was he drunk? Agrees.

THE PROOF

A sabre stuck in the ground. Must be in front of biggest tomb - in centre of cemetery. Sabre to be found in the morning.

CARRYING OUT THE DARE

Ivan buttons up long overcoat because of cold. Enters the cemetery. Encouraged by thoughts of money. Reaches large tomb. Beats sabre into ground. Tries to get up but cannot. Panic.

FROZEN TO DEATH

Next morning, Ivan found by tomb. Frozen to death or killed by nameless horror? Sabre caught in fold of long coat.

Practice work

Read the following story. Make a plan of it, similar to the one for *Cemetery Path* on this page. To make it easier for you, the story has been divided already into its important stages.

Nightmare in Yellow

He awoke when the alarm clock rang, but lay in bed after he'd shut it off, going a final time over the plans he'd made for embezzlement that day and for murder that evening.

Every little detail had been worked out. But this was the final check. Tonight at forty six minutes after eight he'd be free, in every way. He'd picked that moment because this was his fortieth birthday and that was the exact time of day, of the evening rather, when he had been born. His mother had been an astrology fanatic, which was why the moment of his birth had been impressed on him so exactly. He wasn't superstitious himself but it had struck his sense of humour to have his new life begin at forty, to the minute.

Time was running out on him, in any case. As a lawyer who specialised in handling wills, a lot of money passed through his hands – and some of it had passed into them. A year ago he'd 'borrowed' five thousand dollars to put into something that looked like a sure-fire way to double or triple the money, but he'd lost it instead. Then he'd 'borrowed' more to gamble with, in one way or another, to try to recover the first loss. Now he was behind to the tune of over thirty thousand: the shortage couldn't be hidden more than another few months and there wasn't a hope, that he could replace the missing money by that time. So he had been raising all the cash he could without arousing suspicion, by carefully selling property, and by this afternoon he'd have running-away money to the tune of over a hundred thousand dollars, enough to last him the rest of his life.

And they'd never catch him. He'd planned every detail of his trip, his destination, his new identity, and it was foolproof. He'd been working on it for months.

His decision to kill his wife had been relatively an afterthought. The motive was simple: he hated her. But it was only after he'd come to the decision that he'd never go to jail, that he'd kill himself if he was ever picked up, that it came to him that – since he'd die anyway if caught – he had nothing to lose in leaving a dead wife behind him instead of a living one.

He'd hardly been able to keep from laughing at the appropriateness of the birthday present she'd given him (yesterday, a day ahead of time); it had been a new suit-case. She'd also talked him into celebrating his birthday by letting her meet him downtown for dinner at seven. Little did she guess how the celebration would go after that. He planned to have her home by eight forty six and satisfy his sense of fitness of things by making himself a widower at that exact moment. There was a practical advantage, too, in leaving her dead. If he left her alive but asleep, she'd guess what had happened and call the police when she found him gone in the morning. If he left her dead, her body would not be found that soon, possibly not for two or three days, and he'd have a much better start.

Things went smoothly at his office: by the time he went to meet his wife everything was ready. But she dawdled over drinks and dinner and he began to worry whether he could get her home by eight forty six. It was ridiculous, he knew, but it had become important that his moment of freedom should come then and not a minute earlier or a minute later. He watched his watch.

He would have missed it by half a minute if he'd waited till they were inside the house. But the dark of the porch of their house was perfectly safe, as safe as inside. He swung the cosh viciously once, as she stood at the front door, waiting for him to open it. He caught her before she fell and managed to hold her upright with one arm while he got the door open and then got it closed from the inside.

Then he flicked the switch and yellow light leaped to fill the room and, before they could see that this wife was dead and that he was holding her up, all the assembled birthday party guests shouted 'SURPRISE!'

Frederic Brown

Opening paragraphs

In the opening paragraphs you need to say who the main characters are. Describe where the story is taking place and when.
There are special ways of writing these paragraphs.

> You can begin by **describing the area** where the story is to take place so that you suggest the atmosphere.

The Yorkshire moors are strange and lovely places. Sometimes they are soft and gentle. The birds sing and the breezes are kind on your face. But sometimes they are different. They are harsh and cruel, stony and unwelcoming. The wind howls across them, whipping the cold wet rain at you like a knife, slashing through the air. And then there is the mist. The mist falls swiftly and quite silently. Almost at once, with little or no warning, you are lost in a thick white cloud and your sense of direction vanishes unless you know your way about. Lost in the mist, it is like the end of the world. There is no one there.

From *Wild Boy* by Joan Tate

Questions

1 What is meant when the breezes are described as 'kind on your face'? Which other words give the same idea of the breezes?
2 How could the winds be 'stony and unwelcoming'? What does the description 'whipping the cold wet rain at you like a knife, slashing through the air' tell you about the wind?
3 What is the feeling when the mist falls?
4 What general ideas do you get of the moor from this description?
5 Think about this as a setting for a story. What sort of story do you think it is going to be? Why?

You can begin by **surprising the reader** and causing **suspense** by describing something unusual. These are the first few sentences of a story which begins in this way.

I was never particularly keen on my job before the day I got shot and nearly lost it, along with my life. But the ·38 slug of lead which made a pepper-shaker out of my intestines left me with fire in my belly in more ways than one. Otherwise I should never have met Zanna Martin, and would still be held fast in the spider-threads of departed joys, and no use to anyone, least of all myself.

It was the first step to liberation, that bullet, though I wouldn't have said so at the time. I stopped it because I was careless. Careless because bored.

from *The Odds Against* by Dick Francis

Questions

1 What does the writer say in the first sentence to surprise you?
2 The writer gives you some clues about the story here, but leaves many things unexplained. What does he leave you wondering?
3 What sort of story do you think this is going to be?

You can begin in an exciting way. Start at an **important point in the action** of the story.

Brent ran for his life with the sun coming up out of the North Sea behind him, blood-red on the horizon, shafts filtering pale gold to give light to the low grey clouds of the winter sky. He had a start of about two minutes at most.

He was out of the valley now and free, but it would take Stark no longer than two minutes to search for the spy in his ranks, find he was no longer in the cave, and mount the pursuit.

from *Running Scared* by Alan Evans

Questions

1 What is happening to Brent at the beginning of the story?
2 What do you find out about Brent and his past?
3 How would you expect the story to continue?
4 Why is this an exciting introduction to a story?

Here are the beginnings of some stories. Read them carefully. Explain which type of introduction is used in each case.

1

The great bog which lies at the heart of Dartmoor is a silent place. Few birds fly there, and the streams flow quietly between banks of black peat, or lose themselves in morasses of moss and rushes. For many miles you can walk, and hear only the sound of the wind in the heather, and the sullen splash of your own feet in the black water. On a fine, sunny day, this silence is pleasant, a release from the noise of the world; under grey skies, it is grim and threatening.

from *The Wish Hounds* by Kathleen Hunt

2

It was hot in the Number One magistrates court, and after he'd got used to the strangeness of it all, Jim Barker found the whole thing rather boring. The prosecuting solicitor had been droning on for a good ten minutes, and Jim had heard it all a dozen times, of course. He'd never been in the dock before, but he'd been in the witness box – twice. Both times he'd been a witness for the prosecution, and both times the people in the dock had been found guilty, largely due to him. That was just another reason why he knew he had nothing to worry about. He was going to be acquitted.

from *The Common Good* by Jan Needle

3

Cathy stood by the window, her back to the room gazing out across the raggy autumn garden but seeing nothing. The room hadn't been used for days and struck cold and clammy, as if the last week's rains had invaded the house. But Cathy didn't feel it cold; she didn't feel anything. Time had suddenly stopped and she had stopped with it. But she listened. Every nerve of her listened. You could see her listening in the rigid shape of her head held a little back and to one side, hands clenched into tight fists. Morris had to come out of the room some time.

from *A Girl Like Cathy* by Dorothy Clewes

1   Look at the picture. Imagine it is the setting for a story. Write the opening paragraph describing the place and its atmosphere.

2   Choose two of the following titles. Write the opening paragraphs to the stories. Choose a different type of introduction for each story.
One must surprise the reader.
One must begin at an important point in the action.

Escape
The Visitor
The Disaster
The Heat Wave
The Last Day

How to end

There are different ways in which narratives can end. Choose the type of ending most suited to your story.

> You can end in an **expected way**. Make sure that all parts of the story are drawn to a good conclusion. Here is an example of this kind of ending.

It was at that moment that John fully realised that The Bully was not as tough as he had thought. John's shoulder was aching, but he tried not to show it. At the end of the game – which the school team won 28 to 33 – John found himself walking next to Gray without any fears whatsoever. The school ended. John cycled home. The dark cloud which had covered him that morning had completely disappeared. From now on he could go to school without fear or worry about Robert Gray – the bully.

from *First Day at School* by Kevin Prosser, aged 12

Questions

1 What do you think has happened between John and Robert Gray up to this point?
2 How has the situation been sorted out by the end?
3 How have John's feelings changed during the day?

> You can end a story in such a way that the reader is left **a little unsure** about what eventually happened. There could be a sequel to the story. This is called an **open ending**.

'What have you done, Johnny? What have you been up to?'

There was a blinding light inside him, a blinding light that lit up inside from his stomach to his head. He could feel the old man's hands on him. He felt as if his blood had changed into hot steel. He must get away!

His fist closed tighter on the handle of the gasoline can, and he felt his arm swinging out in a high swooping arc. He heard a dull clang. And he felt Bill Trapp become limp.

Johnny ran and ran through the trees. He followed a path lit by the flames. He climbed a tree and swung over the wall. He jumped. He realised he was hurt and bleeding. He ran and ran.

He heard fire engines.

from *Beetle Creek* by William Denby

Questions

1 What had Johnny been up to when Bill Trapp found him?
2 What does Johnny seem to have done to Bill?
3 What does the writer leave you still wondering about at the end of the story?

You can end in a way that **shocks** or **startles** the reader.

'The last spin,' Tigo said. 'Come on, the last spin.'

'Gone,' Dave said. 'Hey, you know, I'm glad that you thought of this idea. You know that? I'm actually glad!' He twirled the cylinder. 'Look, you want to go on the lake on Sunday? I mean with your girl and mine? We could rent two boats. Or even one if you want.'

'Yeah, one boat,' Tigo said. 'Hey, your girl'll like Juana, I mean it. She's a swell chick.'

The cylinder stopped. Dave put the gun to his head quickly.

'Here's to Sunday,' he said. He grinned at Tigo, and Tigo grinned back, and then Dave fired.

The explosion rocked the small basement room, ripping away half of Dave's head, shattering his face. A small, sharp cry escaped Tigo's throat, and a look of incredulous shock knifed his eyes.

Then he put his head on the table and began weeping.

from *The Last Spin* by Evan Hunter

Questions

1 What are Dave and Tigo doing?
2 At first, how does it seem the story is going to end?
3 How does the story end?
4 What is so shocking about the ending?

You can end with an unexpected **twist** to the story where the reader is taken by surprise. This is the way that *Nightmare in Yellow* and *Cemetery Path* end. Read the stories again to see this type of ending.

Practice work

Here are the endings of some stories. Read them carefully and say which type of ending is used in each case. Write a few sentences for each one explaining why.

1

Tick, tick, tick. The grandfather clock made a deafening noise in the stillness of the hall. She sat, too petrified to move, with her back against the wall. She could see every nook and cranny, nothing ... or nobody, could hide.

She felt its presence. The air became stifling, almost smothering her. She fought the idea ... but in vain. Was she to be the last to go?

2

A few yards would take him to the door, and yet David thought he would never get there. His legs could carry him no further and he was on the point of collapsing. He had thought for some time that perhaps if the woman who lived there would tell him what to do and where to go, he would be able to manage, but now he knew he couldn't. If his happiest dreams came true, he could go on living: if not, this was the end.

French was the language he spoke best. David picked up his bundle, walked to the door and rang the bell. When the woman opened it, he knew she was the woman in the photograph, the woman whose eyes had seen so much and yet could smile.

Then David said in French, 'Madame, I'm David. I'm ...' He could say no more. The woman looked into his face and said clearly and distinctly, 'David ... My son, David ...'

from *I Am David* by Anne Holm

3

Len's body circled through the air like a child's golliwog flung petulantly away, and he was hurled against the lorry's radiator with terrifying force, snapping his spine like a matchstick.

'Road hog,' screamed the papers.

'Irresponsible young hooligans,' said he who had never driven more than thirty.

'These young people,' sighed the vicar. 'Too much money and not enough sense.'

'Oh, God,' said the hospital doctor, 'not another.'

Len's mother wept bitterly, hopelessly maintaining to the last that he was a good boy, 'never no trouble'.

A week after the inquest, Sid bought a new bike, a better one.

from *A Five Year Life* by Joan Tate

Practice work

Here is the main part of a story. Read it carefully. Complete the story by writing two possible endings from the four types you now know.

Michael woke with a start. It was still dark. There was a full moon that night, and some of the light filtered through the bedroom curtains. He was able to see the luminous hands of the clock. It was 2.00 am. He looked around the room slowly. He could make out the outline of the wardrobe along the far wall. The chest of drawers near the window took on its familiar shape, as his eyes got used to the dark. What was that by the door? Oh yes – he could make out the dressing gown now. Everything seemed so quiet and still. What had woken him? It was a noise. Where had it come from?

Choosing a style

There are certain ways you can write your essays to make your ideas more interesting.

You can write your story in the style of a **flashback**. You begin with something happening in the present. This makes the main character think about the past. The rest of the essay tells the story of the past. It must come to a suitable ending. The following essay is written in this way. Read it carefully and answer the questions.

A Place of Rest

She was digging the garden when the ground shook with a terrific force. The ever present threat had become reality. In the explosion she had fallen and hit her head on the spade she had been using. She lay unconscious long enough for the radiation to creep like a deadly haze across to the district in which she lived. She woke and the terrible remembrance of what she had seen dawned in her mind. She was far enough away from the house to escape the flying splinters of glass from the windows which had shattered, raining the lawn with millions of pieces of glass.

She already felt strange; her mind was dazed. She found herself lying uncomfortably on the ground. Slowly she made for the potting shed and pulled part of the wall on top of her. The small shed had not been able to withstand the force and it too had collapsed. As the polluted atmosphere began to take over, the white gloss paint blistered and she began to wheeze and choke.

Her mind drifted to the past. She was able to think of her cowardice in a discussion in which she had taken part at school, 'What would you do if you survived a nuclear attack' or something of that nature. She voiced her comments saying she would hope to be killed in the major blast of the bomb and not have to die slowly from the effects of radiation. She recalled saying that if she completely survived, remaining in a nuclear fallout shelter, that she would not like to live when the rest of her family or some other friends were not with her. She and all the others discussed the subject with minor concern, only thinking of it in terms of a very slim possibility. The depressing fact was her parents had most probably been killed. They had been on a shopping trip to Birmingham, an obvious target.

She smelt the dry earth on which she was lying and her wandering mind envisaged the garden before: a place of peace and tranquillity; the smell of dusty sunscorched earth begging for water; flowers blooming in a blaze of vibrant orange, gold and deep crimson; the buzz of busy insects and bees; the chirp of birds. Such lovely memories of a place, destroyed, unable to survive in this alien atmosphere which corroded, ate away at the vulnerable surrounds. The garden was a place in which she used to sit and mull over the happenings of the day.

It was the closest she would be to nature. She could picture the garden in winter covered with a blanket of snow muffling the sound – only children's shrill, echoing voices could be heard. In autumn, a gold brown carpet of leaves clothed with red from the copper-beech could be seen: in spring, row upon row of yellow daffodils and fresh lime green buds on the trees and hedges.

She knew that she, too, had not long to live. Covering herself with the shed panel would only prolong the agony. She felt peaceful; she knew that she would die with the garden she once loved so much. Her mind ebbed away, pain was no longer present, her body was still. The unthinkable, unimaginable had become a reality.

Alison Cooper, aged 15

Questions

1 What happened when the girl was digging the garden?
2 What things which had happened in the past did she think about?
3 How does the story end?

Practice work Choose one of the following and write the essay. Make a plan and prepare a rough draft first.

1

Nothing.

She craned from behind the sheltering screen of laurels to risk a second hasty glance through the scrolls of the tall iron gates to the dusty road beyond. There was no one to spy on her!

Now that the moment had arrived for flight, her courage quailed and dwindled to a pin point. Insoluble problems rose up: craggy mountains that loomed and threatened until she all but turned and fled back into her plaster prison. She put a hand to her constricted throat, and touched the concealed locket.

The memories came flooding back.

from *The Star Trap* by Marjorie Darke

Continue the essay in the style of a **flashback** telling the story of the locket and the memories it brought back.

2

The pilot felt rather than saw that they were losing height. He checked the altimeter – 2000 feet it said reassuringly. That couldn't be right! 'The plane must be lower than that,' he thought. He looked out of the cockpit window. The water was so close he could see the breakers, yet he was a long way from the landing strip. Fear gripped him. He pressed the button for the signal 'Emergency: Fasten Seat Belts', and then tried to regain height. There was no response from the controls. The plane struck the ground with a furious bang. For a while everything went black, but then he came to. 'What on earth happened?' he asked himself.

Write an essay in the style of a **flashback** continuing the story of the plane and its passengers.

Picture *3*

Look at the picture. Imagine you are one of the characters. Write an essay in the style of a **flashback** about what has happened.

You can write a story, which **makes a point** about human behaviour. Here is an essay written in this way. Read it carefully and answer the questions.

The Interview

In the distance I could hear the call of 'Next please'. Slowly I walked towards the dark blue door. The paint shone high and the aluminium handle stood out vividly. The plaque on the door was rectangular and white. Boldly the letters of PJ Brotherstone rose out of the plaque.

I knocked and entered the main room. A slightly balding man sat behind a large leather-topped desk. I gathered this person to be Mr Brotherstone.

'Sit down,' he said without looking up.

I sat down, crossed my legs and folded my arms.

'Your name, please?'

'Robinson, Barbara Robinson.'

Mr Brotherstone looked up. He gazed at me and then past me as if I wasn't there.

'Can I help you?' he said stiffly, still not looking in my direction.

'Yes I've come about the job.'

'What job?'

'The one which you advertised. The secretary's job.'

'That job has already been taken.'

'Why wasn't I told?' I was trying to keep calm. I could feel my tight curls growing tighter on my head. I looked down at my hands, my pinkish palms, dark backs.

Mr Brotherstone continued.

'I don't think that you would be right for the job anyway.'

'And what's that supposed to mean?' I could not control myself any longer. I picked myself up and walked straight out of the door. My head turned. I looked at the closed door behind me, at the white plaque. Why has everything got to be white to be perfect?

Helen Walton, aged 15

Questions

1 In your own words briefly explain the story being told in this essay.
2 What is the point the writer is making about human behaviour?
3 How is this point made?

Practice work

Write a story which **makes a point** about one of the following sorts of human behaviour. Remember to work from a rough to a final draft.

Kindness
Cruelty
Greed
Selfishness
Helpfulness

You can **repeat an idea at important stages** in the story. This gives added meaning. Read the following essay which is written in this way and answer the questions.

Freedom

Dave Trent was a racing driver and a good one at that. Dave raced Formula One cars and was used to winning very regularly. Today would be the last race of his career. After he had taken the chequered flag, and the huge prize, he was going to retire and live the rest of his life in luxury. He was fed up taking risks. He was getting too old; one day he would take a risk that he wouldn't be able to walk away from.

A white butterfly gracefully fluttered past him. His life and career were like that butterfly, he thought. Butterflies didn't live long; neither did his career. He had made more money in the last year than most people make in a lifetime. He compared his early days racing motor-karts to the caterpillar; both were very slow. Today's race was important. It was time to get to his car now. The race was drawing closer.

Sitting safely in his seat with the canopy bolted firmly in place, Dave could hear the massive and powerful engine directly behind him. He was all ready to go. Dave felt good as the car was in tip-top condition. When an adult butterfly emerges, it enters a totally different world. It now has the freedom of flying whenever it wants and much faster than when it had to crawl about. This was like when Dave moved to Formula One cars. The Formula One and the old karts were completely different. With the Formula One Dave had all the speed and power he wanted.

A voice rang out over the pits: 'Will all drivers and cars take their place on the grid, please?' As Dave sat there with all those other drivers he wondered if the light was ever going to change. It was on red for what seemed like an age. Then, suddenly, all Dave's prayers were answered; the lights turned to green and Dave roared away.

He accelerated fast into the first corner. There was just one car in front of him but he wouldn't be too difficult to pass, not for Dave. As they came out of the curve, Dave's vast experience showed as he smoothly went down a gear and accelerated away from the now trailing pack of cars. 'Nobody can catch me now,' thought Dave confidently. Butterflies were free, just like Dave. As Dave came out of the bend into the straight the fantastically powerful engine soon whisked him to over 200 mph. Only a few more seconds and Dave would complete the first lap.

This race was a doddle he thought. He was right as well. There was nobody in the race who could really test him while he was driving this well.

By the tenth lap Dave was getting very tired but that didn't matter now. There was only one lap left and he would have won enough to retire. Dave thought about the butterflies that he had compared his life to, swooping towards flowers. Dave was now swooping towards the chequered flag. There was just one back marker to pass. The slower car obligingly pulled over to give Dave a clear run to the flag, but as Dave passed, the slower car's front wheel came off. He did everything possible to avoid it but it smashed straight into the canopy. The car spun wildly out of control and finally smashed into a barrier. Upon impact, the car burst into flames.

Within seconds the rescue crews were on the spot exting-uishing the flames. They got to Dave and dragged him out and laid him just a few yards from the flaming wreck that was once his most prized possession; his car, the fastest anywhere. The doctor rushed over to Dave and felt for a pulse. There was none. Butterflies do die after all!

Warren Hopley, aged 15

Questions

1 In your own words briefly explain the story being told in this essay.
2 What are the important stages of the story?
3 How does the writer use the butterfly to show these stages?

Practice work

Choose one of the following, and use it in a story to point out the **major stages in the plot**. Look back at *Freedom* to remind your-self how this is done.

The clock
The storm
The garden
The streetlight
The door

Essay work

Look at the following essay questions carefully. To write any of these you need to **use the skills** you have learned so far. Decide on the place, time, and the characters. The plot needs to be planned out. Choose an introduction and conclusion to suit the story. Remember to work from a rough to a final copy.

● Write a story suggested to you by one of these titles.

The Lie
The Survivor
Looking Back
The Stronghold
Number One Court
Nothing to Declare

- Write a story which begins in one of the following ways. Give your essay a title.

  At 4.30 on the afternoon of 20 December, the coastguards reported that there was bad weather blowing in from the sea. By 5 o'clock there were fierce winds and heavy rain over the whole area. The threat of floods was now real.

  She looked at the calendar thoughtfully. It was here at last – her important day.

Picture   Write a story suggested by the following picture.

2 Descriptive writing

To describe an event or place you must have a clear picture of it in your mind. You can then 'paint a picture in words'. Think about what you can see, hear, taste, touch and smell. Give as much detailed information about the scene as you can. Adjectives and comparisons (**similes** and **metaphors**) are useful to describe things vividly.

27

Giving the details

The more detailed a description of a scene is, the more clearly you can 'see' it. In the following extract, the writer gives a detailed description of a rather run-down seaside resort. Read it carefully.

Red Rocks

A long road leads down to the sea, running straight across the sandhills because there are no trees and nothing to turn aside for, and along this road there are a few houses, some in clusters as if afraid of the loneliness, a few bigger ones sturdily on their own. There is also the High Hat Ballroom, which used to be the Rialto Cinema, and there is Owen's Fish and Chip Saloon. Further up, at the T-junction, there is the older and more settled part of the village. Fifty or sixty houses, two pubs and a red-brick church.

For a hundred years or more, Red Rocks has been trying to establish itself as a summer resort. It has the clean, salt sea, it has fresh Atlantic air, and in the little bay it has a half-circle of smooth pale sand, as elegantly rounded as a child's cuticle. At the northern edge of the bay rises the cluster of rocks that gives the place its name, high enough and rough enough for the adventurous big boys of fourteen and fifteen to climb and shout to one another and feel that they're really climbing something. Yes, the place has the makings of a resort. But no more than the makings. A few visitors come in August, a little shanty town of caravans and tents grows up in the field behind Owen's Fish and Chips, but at the beginning of September it all dies down again. Once that cold wind starts whipping across the sand-hills, nobody wants to come near the place. And even in the short season of hot weather, when the sea winks in the sunlight and the rocks feel warm to your hand, most visitors go to the larger resorts down the coast, where there are more amenities.

from *The Life Guard* by John Wain

Questions

1 Use the detailed information given in the passage to draw a sketch map of Red Rocks village.
2 Why is the place called Red Rocks?
3 What does 'as elegantly rounded as a child's cuticle' tell you about the shape of the sandy bay?
4 The writer says that in summer, 'a little shanty town of caravans and tents grows up in the field'. What do 'shanty town' and 'grows up' tell you about the camp site?
5 What are the attractions of Red Rocks for the holiday maker? What are its disadvantages?

Practice work

1 Write a detailed description of the place you live in. Describe what the place looks like. Say what you think are its advantages and disadvantages. Draw a sketch map to go with your work.

Picture

2 Look at the picture carefully. Write a detailed description of this place, in the way John Wain wrote about Red Rocks. Give the place a name.

Using the senses

To describe an event or a place, you need to imagine you are there. Write down what you can see, hear, smell, taste and touch. This will help you bring the scene to life.

In this extract, the writer has used his senses to describe the town he lived in as a child. Read it carefully and answer the questions which follow.

South Shields

The sea was always there, just beyond the piled-up houses and laid out Roman remains. On winter nights, we could hear it roaring, pounding our broad northern beaches. In summer, on sunny holiday afternoons, we could reach it after a short, lingering walk along dazzling, tramcar-shaken Ocean Road, where the spades and pails and beachballs and paper hats and balloons and shrimping nets and sand-shoes and frilly sunshades and dolls and little yachts and celluloid windmills all rattled and whizzed and frivolled outside the postcard emporium and the sandboy toy shops, where they hung in great windy festoons of seaside fun. We would trudge along the sand-strewn pavements, past the privet-scented gates of the South Marine Park and the cat-raked rockeries of the North Marine Park, past the model of the first lifeboat under its Moorish canopy, past the Wouldhave Memorial with its whey-faced clock and chinking iron cups chained to the drinking fountain, past the Mecca Tearooms down to the pier, the promenade, the harbour and the wide, crowded glittering sands. Even at the centre of the town the air had a tang of mint rock and vinegar and seaweed. Here on the beach, tracking through the grimy sand of its street-soiled approaches, the tang was strong and heady with whiffs of laundrylike steam from a little goods engine that chugged from time to time along a rusty, moon-daisied track between the sands and the working town. Sometimes it would pant and fuss along the mile-long pier, which we were always told was the longest in the world. Even in summer, the green North Sea mountained and growled and crashed along the pier's huge grey limestone blocks. Half-way along the dark, oil-dripping, rusty travelling crane reared stiffly, immovably, against a vista of Tynemouth's romantic ruined Priory, the Collingwood Memorial, the gun-emplacements on the cliffs and Tynemouth pier, much shorter and duller than South Shields pier. Our lighthouse was bigger than Tynemouth's stumpy one; it flashed a red light at night, but Tynemouth's light was a common white one. Our lighthouse had a tiny china doll embedded in the cement between two of its great curved blocks: if the storm gates on the pier were open, we could walk right to the end, past the green-stepped boat landings, and rub the china doll for luck.

From the beach, the blinding-white lighthouse appeared to rise bravely out of the shimmering, boat-netting waves. And there, far out on the crisp horizon, the brown-smoked tankers and trawlers trailed, crawling imperceptibly as the hands of the Town Hall clock down the face of the afternoon.

from *The Only Child* by James Kirkup

Questions

1 What did James Kirkup see – as he walked down Ocean Road?
        – as he passed through the Marine Parks?
        – as he walked along the pier?

2 What different noises did he hear as he made his way to the pier?

3 What smells and tastes did he notice most in South Shields?

4 James Kirkup uses words in an interesting way in this extract. Look carefully at the groups of words on page 32. Explain what picture the writer creates in your mind in each group indicated in **bold type**. The first one has been done for you.

'The sea was always there, just beyond **the piled-up houses and the laid out Roman remains**.'

'Piled-up' suggests that the houses were on top of one another, or very close together. It also seems that they were high buildings. This may be because the Roman remains were so low. They had crumbled over the years and were just ruins.

'In summer, on sunny holiday afternoons, we could reach it after a short, lingering walk along **dazzling, tramcar-shaken Ocean Road**'

'past the Wouldhave Memorial with its **whey-faced clock**'

'and the wide, **crowded glittering sands**'

'with whiffs of laundry**like steam from a little goods engine that chugged from time to time**'

'Sometimes it would **pant and fuss along the mile-long pier**'

'the green North Sea **mountained and growled** and crashed along the pier's huge limestone blocks'

'. . . **the blinding-white lighthouse** appeared to rise bravely out of the **shimmering boat-netted waves**.'

'And there, far out on the **crisp horizon**, the brown-smoked tankers and trawlers trailed, **crawling imperceptibly as the hands of the Town Hall clock down the face of the afternoon**.'

Practice work

Picture

Look at the picture.

Make a list of words and phrases connected with what you can see, hear, smell/taste and feel. Draw up four columns as shown here. Write a description of the scene.

What can I see?	What can I hear?	What can I smell/taste?	What can I feel?

Showing the atmosphere

Every event and place has its own particular 'feel' to it. This is called its **atmosphere**.

> Here are two passages which describe the same sort of event – an old lady travelling on a steam train. Read them carefully. You will see that each journey has its own special atmosphere.

The Train Journey

The old lady in the smoking compartment leant forward to look out of the window. She still couldn't see anything, for the window was steamed up and streaked with rain, the night outside as black as soot. Smoke from the engine now and again swirled down round the carriage, making her feel she was being driven through the clouds. Lightning flashed across the sky, for a moment revealing bare wet mountain peaks and thick black pine forests. Then it was dark again, not a single light from a human dwelling to be seen. The train rattled on through the night, the claps of the thunder drowned by the thumpety-thump of the wheels on the train.

The old lady in the smoking compartment leant forward to look out of the window. The windows were crystal clear and she gazed out on a picture-book landscape. White puffs of smoke from the engine, drifted lazily past the carriage making her feel as though she were floating in the clouds. The sun glinted down on the scene. She watched as the slender, silvery birch trees and rich green fir trees flickered past the window like objects in an old film. The sight of the large areas of greenery, and the sapphire blue sky soothed her. There was hardly a human dwelling to be seen in this peaceful setting. Rhythmically the train sped along the tracks, rocking and lulling her as it went.

from *Frankenstein's Aunt* by Alan Petterson

Questions

1   The following words are used to show you the atmosphere of the first passage. Look at the **bold** words. Explain how they make you feel about the scene.

'the night outside as black as soot'

'Smoke from the engine now and again **swirled down round the carriage, making her feel she was being driven through the clouds.**'

'**Lightning flashed across the sky,** for a moment revealing **bare wet mountain peaks and thick black pine forests.**'

'**not a single light from a human dwelling** to be seen'

'**the claps of thunder drowned by the thumpety-thump** of the wheels on the rails'

2   Use the ideas you have collected so far to write a few sentences describing the atmosphere of this scene.

3   Here are some words from the second passage, which help to show its atmosphere. Read them carefully. Describe how they make you feel about the scene.

'The windows were **crystal clear and she gazed out on a picture-book landscape.**'

'White puffs of smoke from the engine, **drifted lazily past** the carriage making her feel **as though she were floating in the clouds.**'

'**trees flickered past the window like objects in an old film**'

'**the sapphire blue sky**'

'the train sped along the track, **rocking and lulling her**'

Write a few sentences describing the atmosphere of the scene.

Practice work

Choose one of the following titles. Write two descriptions of the scene it suggests to you. Give each a different atmosphere.

The Party
Lift Off
November 5th

> The following extract describes an important match which took place between Third Division City East Football Club, and a First Division team called Park Lane. Keith Chapman and his friend Donovan Croft go to see the match. They are supporting opposite sides. Read the extract carefully. It describes the match and its atmosphere.

The Big Day

City East Football Club had risen to the occasion as if it had never been out of the First Division. A new army of turnstile attendants and programme sellers had been recruited and the Metropolitan Police added their own sense of occasion with their proud and frightening police horses. Peanut men and hot dog stands had been attracted to the ground like starlings to bread, and souvenir editions of the evening papers had been specially run off for sale outside the ground. As an all-ticket game it had also attracted its touts, and 'Wanna ticket, gov?' inquiries led to deals of up to five pounds for ninety pence seats. But Mr Chapman had their tickets, and moving inch by inch to their allotted entrance the Crofts and the Chapmans shuffled to the ground.

Keith had never seen so much smoke. It hung in the air above the pitch in a low, hazy cloud as cigarettes were shared and short friendships were made. Its flat greyness gave added colour to the bright and noisy crowd beneath. Donovan's red scarf was out of place at this end of the ground. The big batch of tickets allocated to the Park Lane supporters were all for the entrances at the far end, away from the home team's sometimes violent territory, and already down there the swaying red scarves and jumping heads were competing for attention with the chants of the home supporters.

The two boys leaned on the bar and inhaled the atmosphere, the big occasion, the huge shiver of anticipation which ran over the surface of the crowd.

'Come on, you reds!' came the individual shouts of encouragement. 'We are the champions!' was the proud communal clap, then the whole sea of rolling red and white joined in the modern song of praise.

'When you walk through a storm ...'

City East had a lot of fair-weather support. People who hadn't been to see the team for ages had turned out for the big game. So when the home team ran out to the scratchy sound of 'Blaze Away' they received a huge ovation* too: less organised and melodic but loud enough to lift the hearts of the selected eleven, more varied in appearance than the Park Lane super-squad, two with balding heads, one very young lad on a schoolboy contract, and a tubby goalkeeper, they warmed up with enthusiasm at the near end, the goal they always chose.

The City East goalkeeper cleared a long ball down the middle, a high, hopeful ball which could go to anyone, which the old pro's called 'picking up the pieces'. The opposing centre half would go for it, he would probably win it and head it forward again, while a second wave of the attack ran in ready to snap up the loose ball and get something going. On this occasion it worked. Langton, the City East goalkeeper, used his head well and kicked the ball way up above the level of the stands to drop like a stone deep in the Park Lane half. Peter Wall, the England centre half, big and strong with a long streak of cunning, judged it well and got his head to it, but Fitzwilliam failed to see Pond, the East number nine, hold his shirt and tilt the international off balance. As a result the ball bounced off the top of his head and landed luckily at the feet of Brooks on the City East wing. Park Lane, playing a tight offside game, were square as the slight winger touched it forward to Arthur Morris.

'Offside!' shouted half the ground.

The cry was repeated by four red-shirted players, who stopped immediately and raised their arms in the air, their heads turning as one to the nearer linesman. But to their surprise he held his flag firmly down.

'Play on!' shouted the referee, loudly enough for every man in the ground to hear it, and he waved his arms and high-stepped at speed after the attacking Morris.

* ovation – loud applause

The roar was deafening. The goal was a formality. Even in the Third Division one man can usually beat a goalie left on his own. As Chris Young dived bravely for his feet, Morris scooped the ball up and lobbed it well over the goalkeeper's head to bounce innocently into the net like a baby's beachball.

The crowd went mad.

from *The Trouble with Donovan Croft* by Bernard Ashley

Questions

1 Make a list of the things Keith and Donovan could see, hear and smell as they got near to the football ground. What do they tell you about the atmosphere outside the ground?

2 What could Keith see and hear once he was inside the ground? What do these sights and sounds tell you about the atmosphere there?

3 What were the differences in the way the Park Lane team (the Reds), and the City East team were greeted by the crowd?

4 What was the atmosphere in the ground from the time the ball landed at Brooks' feet, until the goal was scored?

5 The following **bold** groups of words have been used in an imaginative way. Read them carefully. Explain what each group of words helps you to see.

'**A new army** of turnstile attendants and programme sellers **had been recruited**'

'Peanut men and hot dog stands had been attracted to the ground like **starlings to bread**'

'**It hung** in the air above the pitch in a **low, hazy cloud**'

'then the **whole sea of rolling red and white** joined in'

'and kicked the ball way up above the level of the stands to **drop like a stone deep in the Park Lane half**'

'lobbed it well over the goalkeeper's head to **bounce innocently into the net like a baby's beachball**'

Practice work

Picture

Look at the picture carefully. What is the atmosphere? Write a vivid description of it. Show the atmosphere you think it has. Make five columns like those below. Jot down your ideas in them. Now write your essay.

What can I see?	What can I hear?	What can I smell/taste?	What can I feel?	What is the atmosphere?

Using adjectives and comparisons

Adjectives are describing words. They tell you about the shape, size, colour, type, and condition of things. In **similes** and **metaphors** one thing is compared with another. This helps the reader to picture it more clearly. In a simile the word 'like' is used. Adjectives and comparisons help to make descriptive writing vivid.

> In this extract the writer uses simple adjectives to give a clear description of a room. Jamie visits Julie's flat for the first time. This is what he sees.

Julie's Room

In one corner was a writing bureau with a lamp next to it that had a red shade. The shade matched red cushions on the white settee which had its back to a wall of green wallpaper. Near the window, where big yellow curtains were drawn, was an armchair that matched the settee. In front of the settee was a coffee table upon which was a portable typewriter and two folders. Standing on the folders was a stem glass of sherry. At the same end of the room as the bureau, only in the other corner was a television set turned on with the volume low. The carpet was a red wall-to-wall carpet and there was a white rug before the fireplace. An electric fire shot heat across the room and a lamp was shinning on the typewriter which had a half-typed page in it. A cosy, dimly lit smart room, Jamie thought.

from *Green Leaves of Nottingham* by Pat McGrath

Questions

1 Make two columns like those which follow.

Object	Adjective
bureau	writing
lampshade	red
cushions	
settee	

In the first column, make a list of the objects Jamie sees in the room. In the second column, write down the adjectives which describe them. Some examples have been done for you.

2 The writer says that the 'electric fire shot heat across the room'. What does the word 'shot' suggest about the heat?

3 What general feelings did Jamie have about the room?

Practice work

Write a description of your own room, or a room you would like for yourself. Draw up two columns as on page 40 before you begin writing. In the first column, list all the important things in the room. In the second column, jot down one or two adjectives to describe each of the objects. Use these ideas to write a clear description of the room you have chosen.

In this description of a kitchen, the writer uses more complicated adjectives. This gives a fuller picture of the room and its atmosphere.

Mrs Battey's Kitchen

There were so many new things to look at in her kitchen. She had a bed that folded up into a mahogany cupboard. Did she call it a 'dess bed', or did I not hear her aright? Her 'clippy' mats had a different texture from ours; they had weird, straggling patterns on them, and she wasn't as fond as my mother of 'mixy-maxy' centres. Her tablecloth was of wine-coloured velours, with a deep tasselled fringe round the edge, whereas ours was a faded pink cotton one, edged with strawberry-shaped bobbles.

The patterns on her wallpaper and canvas floor covering were extraordinarily different from ours; I thought they were too strange and hideous for words, but I never said so. The wallpaper in Mrs Battey's kitchen had a brownish background covered with a pattern of dull red and eggy-yellow leaves and pale fawn flowers which Mrs Battey proudly identified as 'Dusty Millers'. The canvas on the floor had a dizzy pattern of green lilies and purple grapes on imitation brown tiles with an orange-squiggled border. It was an interlocking pattern, and my eyes would become dazed and weary as I tried obsessively to understand its tortured, meaningless logic.

It was always stiflingly hot in her little kitchen for she liked to keep a good fire going even in the height of summer. Her fire-irons, brass fender and black-leaded 'fire tidy' round the ashpan were clean and shining, just like my mother's downstairs. She, too, whitewashed her hearth afresh every morning after raking out the ashpit and the flues. The oven door of her kitchen range was exactly the same as ours, but the design of the little ventilator-windows that slid open or shut at the top was not quite the same as ours. I liked opening and shutting those tiny windows, even when the little knob on the shutter was almost too hot to touch; and sometimes I got into trouble for opening them when my mother had a batch of scones baking in the oven. I didn't dare touch Mrs Battey's oven-ventilator: I was sure it would be too hot to hold; the heat of her enormous fire made the oven tick and rattle alarmingly, and whenever she opened the oven door she used an 'oven cloth'. How she clashed the door.

from *The Only Child* by James Kirkup

Questions

1 Why did the writer find Mrs Battey's kitchen interesting?
2 Which words does the writer use to describe the patterns on Mrs Battey's 'clippy mats'?
3 How was Mrs Battey's tablecloth different from his mother's?
4 Describe Mrs Battey's wallpaper and canvas floor covering. How did the writer feel about them? Which adjectives tell you?
5 What was the atmosphere like in the kitchen? Why was it like this?
6 What did the writer see around Mrs Battey's hearth? What did they show about her?
7 Why was the writer afraid of Mrs Battey's oven?
8 What were his general feelings about the kitchen?

Practice work   Choose one of the following.

Picture

1   Look at the picture. Write a vivid description of the room and the objects in it. Use as many adjectives as you can to describe everything in detail. Remember to describe the shapes, sizes, colours, types and conditions of the things you can see.

2   **It was the most unusual room I had ever seen.**
     Write a suitable description of a room and the things in it.

These following extracts describe areas in different towns. Read them and answer the questions.

Here is a description of Cassie's first visit to Strawberry.

Strawberry

Strawberry was nothing like the tough, sprawling bigness I had envisioned. It was instead a sad, red place. As far as I could see, the only things modern about it was a paved road which cut through its centre and fled northward, away from it, and a spindly row of electric lines. Lining the road were strips of red dirt splotched with patches of brown grass and drying mud puddles, and beyond the dirt and mud puddles, gloomy store buildings set behind raised wooden sidewalks and sagging verandahs.

As the stores gave way to houses still sleeping, we turned onto a dirt road which led past more shops and beyond to a wide field dotted with wooden stalls.

from *Roll of Thunder, Hear My Cry* by Mildred D. Taylor

Questions

1 What did Cassie think the town would be like?
2 Which adjectives tell you what it was really like?
3 What were the only modern things she could see in Strawberry?
4 What did the buildings look like to her?
5 Read these phrases carefully. Explain what each of the **bold** words suggests.
  'a paved road which **cut** through its centre and **fled** northward'
  'a wide field **dotted** with wooden stalls'
6 How did Cassie feel about the town? Which adjectives tell you?

This extract describes an area of London during the war.

The Bombed Street

Lucas moved, slipping down an alley between a split corrugated-iron fence and catwalking a broken wall. At the end was a nightmare landscape, a burning wasteland where nothing remained untouched. Through a hole between gaping walls he saw shuttered warehouses, isolated chimneys, a glimpse of brackish water, toppled cranes. Nearer, a bucket and chain gang was working at the end of the wrecked street, scooping water that gushed from the broken main. Fire glowed, billowing flames and smoke, lighting a pub from within spitting out sparks and hot slivers of glass. Nearer still, a terrace of houses leaned together in a drunken pyramid wreathed round by heaps of brick and wood. A small group of people were burrowing there.

from *A Long Way to Go* by Marjorie Darke

Questions

1   Make two columns like those which follow.

Objects	Adjectives
fence wall	split, corrugated-iron

In the first column, list the objects Lucas saw as he walked through the bombed area. In the second column, list the adjectives used to describe each object. Some examples have been done for you.

2   The writer uses these comparisons to show you what Lucas saw. Explain what each comparison tells you about the scene.
'At the end was a **nightmare landscape**'
'a terrace of houses **leaned together in a drunken pyramid**'
'**wreathed round by** heaps of brick and wood'

Practice work

Picture

Look at the picture of the street scene. Write a description of it using adjectives and comparisons. Use any adjectives from this section which are suitable, as well as others of your own.

Using verbs, adverbs and comparisons

Verbs are words which describe **actions**. **Adverbs** tell you **how** the actions are done. Read the following extract carefully.

The Footballer

The footballer ran on to the pitch quickly. He carried the ball safely under his arm as he strode proudly to his position in the centre of the field. He placed the ball carefully on the ground and stepped backwards cautiously. He looked around him eagerly, as he was keen to start. The whistle blew shrilly. He darted forward speedily and kicked the ball firmly. The game was under way.

Draw up two columns like those below.

Verbs	Adverbs
ran	quickly

In the first column, write down the verbs which describe what the footballer does. In the second column, write down the adverbs which describe how those actions were done. An example has been done for you.

Verbs and adverbs describe actions. They can also make a piece of description exciting to read. The following extract shows this.

> Emily is in a protest march. The police try to break it up. This is what happens.

The Protest March

The main gates were already closed and locked. No use bothering with those, but one of the side gates had not yet been fastened. Already some of the women were climbing on the railings, pushing and shoving, struggling to get through. Indian clubs whirled among the encroaching mob. From being a well-ordered procession they were divided into small groups. Elbowing with all her might, Emily pushed forward, helped by the pressure of bodies from behind. One of the police horses was edging towards her, its great piebald haunches moving sideways, the rider shouting:

'Closed! No way through.'

'Get hold of her, Jack . . . throw her this way.'

She felt her collar grabbed and was flung towards her tormentor, but not before she had jabbed an elbow with some force into the unseen Jack's stomach. She heard him grunt and was saved from the blow aimed at her by being shoved headlong into a mass of heaving bodies. There was no time for thought. All principles about no violence were lost in a desperate need. for self-preservation. Handbags, truncheons and clubs met flesh in agonising blows. One crunched on her shoulder, sending tingling pain to her fingertips. She felt her voice shout obscenities that were lost in the yells and screams buffeting her ears. There was anger in her now, a bursting fury that needed expression, but crushed as she was against the lathering flank of a police horse it was all she could do to prevent herself from being trampled underfoot. She glimpsed a hat skimming the air. The horse flicked its tail and as it danced sideways, a woman, armed with a pair of secateurs, cut through the bridle. The rider swore, kicking out as he dismounted and scoring Emily's cheek. The pain dug through her head and, hand to face, she was distantly surprised to feel blood oozing between her fingers.

The gap closed and the crowd shifted, knocking her off her feet. She did not fall. Tight-packed bodies pinioned her arms, wringing the breath from her lungs. Her hat had gone and her hair tumbled free. Another shift. Fists punched. A horse neighed above the howls of the mob, and helplessly Emily was sucked down into a sea of bodies which closed over her head. Her courage died as light was shut out. Sheer panic doubled her strength, but several hundredweight of flesh and bone pressed her relentlessly down. In the jungle of trouser legs, torn skirts and thudding boots there was no escape and her shouts for help were choked in tweed and flannel. Trodden and kicked, her hair hooked on buttons and torn from her head, she would have been lost if the tide of movement had not changed. There were shouts of: 'Someone's down ... look out for the woman ... mind yer feet,' as a policeman guided his horse to divide the crowd.

from *A Question of Courage* by Marjorie Darke

Questions

1 What did the women do when they found the gates locked?
2 What did Emily try to do and how did the police stop her?
3 What happened to her after she was thrown into the crowd?
4 Why is the description of the whole incident exciting?
5 The following **bold** words have been used in an interesting way. Explain what each of them suggests.

'yells and screams **buffeting** her ears'

'The pain **dug** through her head'

'Tight-packed bodies **pinioned** her arms, **wringing** the breath from her lungs.'

'helplessly, Emily was **sucked** down into a sea of bodies'

'In the **jungle** of trouser legs, torn shirts and thudding boots'

6 Draw up five columns like those which follow.

Emily	Women	Crowd	Police	Horses

Find words from the extract which tell you about the movements of each of these. Write them down in the correct column.

Practice work   Some of the verbs and adverbs have been left out of the following passages. Rewrite the passages putting in verbs and adverbs to describe actions. Use words from the lists you have made. Add any other suitable words you can think of. You can put more than one word in a space.

A Count of Nine

(Nick finds himself fighting Powell, the ABA champion, in a boxing match.)

Nick ———— from his corner to confront Powell, who ———— his left glove in brief salute. For a few seconds they ———— the ring without either man delivering a blow. Then Nick ———— to his right, feinted to the body and went in with a fast double left jab. The first was fractionally short of its target but the second ———— on Powell's mouth. The ABA champion immediately —— —— with a left hook, ———— with breathless speed into the ribs. Nick grunted but did not retreat. He ———— another double jab with the left and followed with a right to the solar plexus, which Powell ———— with his elbow and ———— his own right to Nick's head. It was a short punch, perfectly timed, and it ———— ———— Nick's left jaw. Nick's skull instantly flooded with crimson darkness, his legs ———— and a couple of seconds later, as full consciousness returned, he found that he was on his hands and knees upon the canvas. He shook his head like a dog emerging from a pond. He could hear the referee intoning the passing seconds: '. . . four . . . five . . . six . . . seven . . .'. At the count of eight he was on one knee and at nine he was back on his feet.

from *A Lonely Game* by Vernon Scannell

The Riot

There was a hush – everyone stopped talking and breathing at the same time – then as though a rubber band had been cut, bodies shot out of everywhere at the same time.

One shout heaved to the heavens, and like a roaring wave, bodies ——————— against me, ——————— me backwards, ——————— me off my feet, yet ——————— me upright by sheer numbers, the pressure of movement. Policemen on horseback ——————— into them, swinging clubs, policemen on foot ——————— and broke up the wall of human flesh into smaller, more manageable knots. My support gone, I fell to the sidewalk. Feet ——————— over me, people ——————— and fell, pulled themselves up and rushed to join whatever was going on over my head. Twice I tried to ——————— to my feet, was ——————— down and ———————, holding both hands over my head – my elbows meeting in front of my face – terrified, knowing that I would be ——————— to death by the sightless mob.

from *The Friends* by Rosa Guy

This extract describes the movement of a machine – a spaceship. Keill Radnor is flying a shuttle back to his spaceship. He is attacked by his enemies from Veynaa. His friend Glr comes to his rescue.

The Veynaan Attack

Hands flashing over the controls, Keill cut power and brutally forced the nose of the ship down. It fell away, twisting and fishtailing – as five energy beams blazed through the space it had vacated.

At once Keill slammed on full power and jerked the ship again, its drive howling, its own beam raking upwards.

Bright flame exploded from the sterns of the two ships in the middle of the attacking group. As they faltered, Keill flashed between them, neatly intersecting the path of the attackers.

51

The two damaged ships spiralled away. Keill ignored them, knowing that they were only disabled, and should reach the planet safely if the pilots were good enough. He dragged to ship over in a tight loop, his eyes blurring darkly for a moment as the gravs clutched him, the ship shuddering and vibrating in protest. The three remaining Veynaans had also begun to wheel, in a gentler curve, but then frantically tried to twist round to bring their guns to bear as they found Keill sweeping down on top of them.

Before they could find their aim, Keill's gun fired again, slashing into the body of one of the ships – which whirled crazily away, out of control.

In the same moment, thundering out of the emptiness, Glr was there, the forward guns of Keill's fighter ablaze.

One of the two remaining Veynaan ships jerked upwards, as if it had run into an invisible wall. Keill felt rather than heard the explosion as flame gushed from a gaping rent in its hull.

from *Deathwing over Veynaa* by Duncan Hill

Questions

1 Which words tell you about Keill's ship?
2 Which words describe the actions of the Veynaan ships?
3 Make four columns like those which follow.

Quick	Slow	Smooth	Jerky

Read through the lists of words you have made. Decide if the actions being described are quick, slow, smooth or jerky. Jot down the words in the correct columns. Add any other suitable words you can think of.

Practice work

In the following extract, the girl is in fear of her life. Although she cannot drive she is attempting to escape by car. Rewrite the passage filling in the spaces. Make the description of the actions interesting.

Pursued

The tyres _____ on the damp grass of the verge – which was just as well or she would have _____ straight into the hedge – and, a miracle, she found herself _____ half on the road and half on the grass.

Trying to keep the speed the same was not too difficult as she was not only fixed in first gear, but also had the hand-brake still on. Steering became the main problem. She _____ the wheel and _____ the grass verge just in time as a tree _____ in front, but then found herself on the opposite side of the road. _____ from the ditch on that side brought her back to _____ against the verge on the other. It was very dark in spite of the moonlight, particularly where trees overhung the road, but she couldn't spare a hand to feel around for a light switch, and certainly wasn't going to risk stopping.

Several times she cried out as the shadowy hedge _____ to her, and at times she took her foot off the accelerator _____ a threatened _____ into a ditch, only _____ forward again as she _____ the car onwards. Suddenly she was shocked to see a hedge, apparently right across the road in front of her.

At that moment a car, _____ along the main road, illuminated the scene with its great swath of headlights. She had reached the junction.

Quite unable to brake, Jo _____ the steering wheel round and, with a squeal of tyres and a sure feeling that the Mini was going _____ over, she found herself actually on the main road and following the vanishing tail lights of the other car.

from *The Silbury Triangle* by David Churchill

Practice work Describe a journey on one of the following forms of transport:

helicopter	sailing boat	racing car
Jumbo jet	taxi	ocean liner
horse and cart	canoe	

Essay work The following questions will give you a chance to **use the skills** you have learned so far. To write an interesting description of any one of these scenes, make sure that you have a clear 'picture' of it in your mind. Then use your senses to give you all the ideas you need. Remember to use **adjectives, verbs, adverbs** and **comparisons.**

1 The time was ten past eight. The cause of the upheaval was a bright glow in the night sky with leaping flames and flying sparks, and I knew at once and without hope that the place on fire was mine.

Describe the scene and what the narrator feels.

2 The shop that filled me with awe was quite small. It was tucked away between two much bigger ones, and as well as the usual broken glass it had a barrier of warped and rusted metal in front of it. When I looked in it was like Aladdin's cave.

Decide what sort of shop this can be. Imagine that you enter the shop. Describe what you find in there in detail.

3 There was rain and fog that Monday morning with the street light and the lit shop windows groping with tentacles of light in the smelly mist.

Write a description of the town centre. Show the effect the rain and fog have on the colours to be seen.

4 Write a description of a pop concert or a disco.

3 Character writing

Characters need to be described in a clear and interesting way. Show what type of people they are by using adjectives and comparisons. Describe what they look like and what they do. Sometimes characters will cause what happens in the story.

Using adjectives

> You can describe your characters in a straightforward way by using adjectives. Read the following extract carefully.

Okonwo

Okonwo was now nearly forty years old. His fame had grown like a bush fire and he was very famous indeed. He was tall and big and he walked like someone with springs in his feet. He had thick black eyebrows over his nose. His nose was wide. If you did not know Okonwo, and if you just looked at him, you would think he was a serious man and not very kind to people.

Sometimes Okonwo would be very angry. When he was angry, Okonwo could not say what he wanted to say. So he used his hands instead of words, and he hit people.

Okonwo's father died ten years ago. His father was called Unoka. Unoka was a very lazy person and he did not like work. He did not like seeing blood and he was afraid of fighting. Unoka had been poor all his life because he never saved any money.

When Unoka had some money he always spent it on lots of palm wine. He asked all his friends to come to his hut and drink the wine with him. They used to have a very happy time, sitting in a circle, drinking and singing songs. He was a sad-looking man and only seemed to be happy when he was making music. Music made Unoka very happy.

Okonwo was ashamed of his father. Okonwo hated men who were lazy. And, as he was strong and brave, he hated men who were afraid of fighting in battles and wars.

When Unoka died, he left nothing for his wife and children. Okonwo wanted to be strong and rich and powerful but he began with nothing. In the village it was not important who your father was. People knew that Okonwo would do great things.

from *Things Fall Apart* by Chinua Achebe

1   Now draw up two columns like those below. In the first column, make a list of the adjectives the writer uses to describe what Okonwo **looks like.** In the second column, write the adjectives the writer uses to describe what kind of **characters** Okonwo and Unoka have. One example of each is done for you.

ADJECTIVES	
Describing appearance	Describing character
Tall, black (eyebrows)	Serious

2   Think of adjectives which could be used instead of each of the following. Add them to your columns.
'So he used his hands instead of words, and he hit people.'
'He did not like seeing blood'
'he was afraid of fighting'
'he never saved any money'
'He asked all his friends to come to his hut and drink the wine with him.'

Practice work

Pictures

Look carefully at the pictures of two different characters. Jot down words to describe each one's appearance and character. Think of a place they could meet and why they should be together. Describe their meeting. Use as many adjectives as you can to describe the appearance and character of each person.

Describing appearance

You can describe people's physical appearances in such a way as to suggest what kind of character they are.

Read the following extracts and answer the questions.

Craggy Face

After being searched they went to a small lounge where passengers for their flight were gathering. Goldenrod noticed two men talking intently together. The younger of them was wearing a light grey suit; he was tall and thin, with dark hair smarmed down with too much lotion. But it was his glittering coal-black eyes that caught Goldenrod's attention. They were cruel and cold, and one thing was certain: those eyes would never smile. The older man was quite different. Ill-at-ease in a crumpled blue suit, he looked like a retired boxer. He had a thick-set body, a craggy face with a big nose that had been badly broken and dull glazed pale blue eyes. Although he was obviously much stronger than the younger man, it was clear who was the dominant personality – Craggy Face – as Goldenrod christened him, was listening to every word the other man said.

from *Goldenrod* by Jim Slater

Questions

1 In your own words describe each of the men's physical appearance.
2 What kind of character is suggested by each description?

Practice work

Write a vivid, detailed description of a person which ends with one of the following sentences. Make sure you describe physical appearance (build, dress etc.) and suggest character.

It was the face of a murderer!
She was a beautiful, innocent child.
But around his eyes, you could tell he was definitely afraid.

Describing actions

The way people move and act can show their characters. Use suitable verbs and adverbs to describe their actions.

In the following extract, the writer describes two wrestlers and their seconds getting ready to start a match. Read it and answer the questions.

Shmule versus 'The Python'

A little wiry man in shirt sleeves and braces came bounding up the aisle, and leaped into the ring. After him marched the wrestlers.

First Shmule, in a crimson dressing gown gleaming in the light, with Blackie and Oliver bustling round him. A man leaned over to pat his back as he passed and when he sprang into the ring there was quite a big cheer. Shmule bowed towards the cheers and looked proudly at the small group who booed. He waved to Joe and Joe waved back.

After him came the dreaded Python with his manager, a man with a square blue jaw, like polished rock. The Python wore a black silk dressing gown and a white towel round his neck, and he towered above the seconds dancing around him. He climbed into the ring, not so full of spring as Shmule but with one powerful hitch of his arm.

The MC introduced Shmule first. He called him the white hope of Aldgate, the sensational young former amateur championship contender, a cleanfighting local boy, and so on and so forth. All the while The Python was baring his teeth and growling and shaking his fist at Shmule's supporters. Shmule slipped out of his crimson dressing gown and now his muscles rippled in the ring lights, his spotless white hammer emblem shining like a star against the crimson briefs. Oliver and Blackie clustered round his corner with towels and pails and a chair for him to sit on between rounds.

The dreaded Python Macklin was very angry. He strained like a fierce bulldog at the rope, just waiting for the bell to sound to throw himself on Shmule, tearing him limb from limb like the Christian martyrs, just as Mavis said. The black hair on The Python stood up in fury and he ground his teeth together. When the MC pointed in his direction and called out his name, famous contender for the championship of the world, and veteran of the ring all over Europe, The Python drew himself up and the muscles on his chest and back were swollen with pride and power. He grinned, his teeth clamped tight together, and when the red-haired woman screamed out, 'Murder him, Py,' he stared at her as if he was hungry and she was a juicy steak.

from *A Kid for Two Farthings by* Wolf Mankowitz

Questions

1 Which two verbs describe the way the referee arrives in the hall? What impression of the referee do these words give you?
2 Describe how Shmule enters the ring, and what he does when he gets there. What do these actions show about his character?
3 What do the two wrestlers do while the MC is introducing Shmule? What impression of their characters do you get?
4 Which words are used to describe the actions of Shmule's and The Python's seconds. What do they suggest about these people?
5 What do the following tell you about The Python?
'He strained like a fierce bulldog on a rope'
'he ground his teeth together'
'he stared at her as if he was hungry and she was a juicy steak'

Practice work
Picture

Look carefully at the picture of a busy street. Study one of the people closely. Write a description of him or her as he or she walks across the road and past the shops. Use verbs and adverbs to show the character very clearly.

Describing habits and mannerisms

One way of showing a person's character is to describe any special habits or mannerisms he or she has. The following extracts show you how to do this. Read them carefully.

Miller, plump and short, several years the younger; tuft of corn-coloured hair and a round, choir boy's face: often his lips quivered and he had a mannerism of putting both hands to his mouth and nibbling at his nails.

from *The Cage* by Roy Brown

Willie was Matty's senior by three months. He was as tall as Matty but without his sturdiness, being very thin with a long lugubrious* face. Nothing about Willie inspired confidence, or gave evidence of stability. He had the nervous habit of twitching his nose, very much like that of a rabbit. Moreover, when he got excited he stammered.

from *Matty Doolin* by Catherine Cookson

*lugubrious – sad, gloomy

I thought Miss Bates the gonest*: six feet tall, thin, with pretty teeth that shone when she did that slow pull back of her thick lips to the laugh lines at the sides of her mouth. She had mixed grey hair, bunned at her neck; always wore two-piece outfits of soft wool, in different colours, which seemed made to fit her long, lanky frame. And she always wore one strand of pearls. My name for her from the first: El-e-gant.

I had a picture of her eyes drawn in my head: two pools of melted tar, beneath which the sun had sunk.

from *Edith Jackson* by Rosa Guy

* gonest – the best

Questions

1 What is each character's habit or mannerism?
2 What do these tell you about the kind of person he or she is?

Practice work

Picture

Study the following pictures carefully. Think of the kind of character each person might have. Think of their particular habits or mannerisms. Now write a good, vivid description of each one. Show their characters through these habits and mannerisms.

Using comparisons

You can describe character by using comparisons. Compare the person's appearance, movements, speech or habits with something which will suggest their character. Your comparisons must be lively and original.

Find the comparisons in the following extracts.

1   With her fair frizzy hair, her baby-blue eyes, and her rose-pink silk dress embroidered with silver, she looked as sweet as sugar icing.

2   Coming down the street, towering over everyone, like some giant in a fairy story, gesticulating with his hands and arms and shoulders as he talked, showing off his well-tailored grey suit with its diamond tie pin glittering in the sun, strode Calvin.

3   His wife was small and gentle and she reminded Robert of a little furry creature, a mouse or a mole.

4   The youngest was the last to leave. He had a mop of fair hair and the face of an angel. He was laughing merrily.

5   The headmaster gave a weird smile, like a copper who's caught you bunging bricks or something.

Draw four columns like those below. In column two, say what it is about the character which is being described in each extract. In column three, say what it is being compared with. In the fourth column, say what is suggested by the comparison. One example is done for you.

Extract number	Character	Compared with	Suggests
1	fair hair, blue eyes and pink dress	icing sugar	sweetness, pleasantness

Practice work   Fill in the table below with lively and original comparisons. One example is done for you.

Characteristic	Comparison
Angry, violent amusing, jovial easygoing old, miserable lonely tall, powerful small, delicate mean lively, friendly hardworking cunning	He exploded like an erupting volcano.

Choose one of these types of character. Write a paragraph describing that person's appearance, movements and speech by using comparisons. Remember that you are trying to show what type of character he or she is.

Using speech

> You can show character through what a person says and how he or she says it. You need to use verbs of saying. Make sure you set out the speech in the correct way. Read the following extracts.

Grandad

When it did he found himself looking into the stomach of a large brown-faced, grey-haired man with enormous hands and very white teeth. A kind of roar came out of the mouth and the hands clutched his ribs and heaved him into the air.

'Markie boy,' thundered the voice. 'I'm your old grandad and welcome home.' He was given the squeeze of a python and then set down. 'Merle,' shouted his grandfather. 'Here's the boy.'

from *A Tide Flowing* by Joan Phipson

Questions

1 Which words tell you how Grandad spoke?
2 What do they suggest about the kind of person he is?
3 What do they suggest about his attitude to the boy?

Miss Gottlieb

Miss Gottlieb was a remarkably ugly woman, partly from her affliction and partly because she had never been beautiful. But although her left side was dead, both her eyes were alive – brilliant, black and beady, shining with hatred, which she directed at her students – most of whom were black and Puerto Rican. Her good-morning greeting to them was a sneer that spread her ugliness far beyond her face to embrace the room.

from *Ruby* by Rosa Guy

Questions

1 Describe how Miss Gottlieb says good-morning to the pupils?
2 What does this tell you about her character and attitude?

Direct speech

You must be careful to punctuate speech properly. There are certain rules which you must learn and use. Study the following diagram.

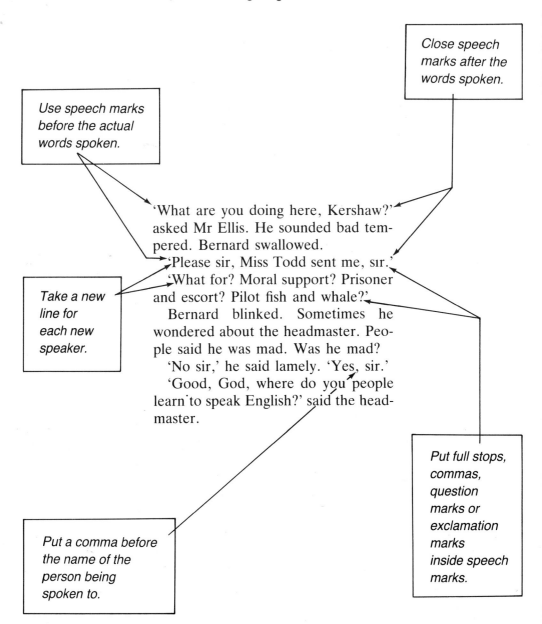

Close speech marks after the words spoken.

Use speech marks before the actual words spoken.

'What are you doing here, Kershaw?' asked Mr Ellis. He sounded bad tempered. Bernard swallowed.
'Please sir, Miss Todd sent me, sir.'
'What for? Moral support? Prisoner and escort? Pilot fish and whale?'
Bernard blinked. Sometimes he wondered about the headmaster. People said he was mad. Was he mad?
'No sir,' he said lamely. 'Yes, sir.'
'Good, God, where do you people learn to speak English?' said the headmaster.

Take a new line for each new speaker.

Put a comma before the name of the person being spoken to.

Put full stops, commas, question marks or exclamation marks inside speech marks.

Use a **variety** of verbs of saying. These will describe how a person says something and suggest what kind of person he or she is. What is the difference in attitude of the following speakers?

> ' I can't wait,' he wailed.
> ' I can't wait!' he roared.
> ' I can't wait,' he sighed.
> ' I can't wait,' he sneered.

Draw up five columns. Fill in five verbs of saying of each type. One of each is done for you.

Quiet verbs	Angry verbs	Answering verbs	Questioning verbs	Humorous verbs
whispered	shouted	replied	demanded	laughed

Practice work Study the following cartoon carefully. Write a description of what is happening. Use direct speech for the actual words spoken. Use suitable verbs of saying and make sure that the punctuation is correct. Look back at the example on page 70 to remind you.

Practice work   Read the following extract and fill in suitable verbs and adverbs of saying.

'Pardon?'

'I think you heard,'

'Apples?'

'That's right. They're a kind of fruit.' I was getting extremely agitated.

'Hey, now wait a minute. . . .'

'Presumably there is someone to whom I may speak about this, or should I take the complaint to the Civil Authority?'

He didn't smile any more after that.

'Is this an official complaint or a private one?'

'Obviously private – they are my apples,'

'Where do you keep these apples?'

'They are growing in my garden.' He seemed to be doing all the questioning. I'm not very good at this sort of scene.

Read the following extract. Write a detailed **character study** of Edith. Say what you find out about her character from her **appearance**, her **actions** and **habits** and **what she says**.

Edith

Her name was Edith.

I did not like her. Edith always came to school with her clothes unpressed, her stockings bagging about her legs with big holes, which she tried to hide by pulling them into her shoes but which kept slipping up, on each heel, to expose a round, brown circle of dry skin the size of a quarter. Of course there were many children in the class that were untidy and whom I did not like. Some were tough. So tough that I was afraid of them. But at least they did not have to sit right across the aisle from me. Nor did they try to be friendly as Edith did – whenever she happened to come to school.

Edith walked into the classroom at late morning causing the teacher to stop in the middle of one of her monotonous sentences to fasten a hate-filled glare, which Edith never saw, on her back.

'Good afternoon, Miss Jackson.' The teacher's voice, thick with sarcasm, followed her to her seat. But Edith, popping bubble gum on her back teeth so that it distorted her square little face, slammed her books on the desk, slipped her wiry body into her seat, then turned her head around the room nodding greetings to friends.

The teacher's voice rose sharply: 'It seems to me that if you had to honour us with your presence today, you could at least have been preparing yourself to come to class looking presentable.'

Her words had more effect on the class than on Edith. They always did. When I had first come into class I had thought it was because the teacher was white. Later I realised that it was because of the manner she spoke to the pupils. Now, the shuffle of the feet sounded around the room, a banging of desks. The teacher shrilled; 'I am talking to you, Edith Jackson.'

'Huh, what? – oh, you talking to me? Good afternoon, Miss Lass.' Edith grinned with open-faced innocence. The teacher reddened. Edith turned her impish grin to include all of the appreciative snickers around the room. She had leaned across the aisle and said to me: 'Hi ya doin', Phillisia?'

I pulled myself tall in my seat, made haughty little movements with my shoulders and head, adjusted the frills on the collar of my well-ironed blouse, touched my soft, neatly plaited hair and pointedly gave my attention to the blackboard.

Edith ignored my snub. She always ignored my snubs. Edith had made up her mind from the first day I entered this class that she would be my friend whether I wanted it or not. 'Ain't it a pretty day out?' She grinned and made a loud explosion with her gum.

from *The Friends* by Rosa Guy

Using character in story

So far you have looked at ways of describing character in a lively, original way. You can also use character in your narrative essays. You can **build the plot** around the characters. The story is caused by the type of people they are. The following story shows you how this is done.

The Old Flame

To commit a murder on a bank holiday at a popular seaside resort in broad daylight argues a good deal of courage, of a sort; but courage was the one quality in which Jack Saunders was not deficient.

In fact, when he began to make his plans for the elimination of Maggie, he soon realised that the boldest course was the safest.

In some ways he genuinely regretted the necessity of what he was about to do, but once he had recognised that Maggie was an insurmountable obstacle to his career, he firmly put any useless repining at one side.

A phrase from a bit of poetry learned by heart at school – that must have been in the last term before he was expelled – came faintly back to his memory. Something about rising on stepping stones of our dead selves to higher things. It seemed oddly appropriate – with this important difference, that it was on the stepping stone of Maggie's dead self that he proposed to rise.

As to the higher things – they, of course, were represented by Mary Rossiter – Mary and her money and her absurdly gullible family, who had taken him at his face value and accepted him as Mary's fiancée without making the smallest inquiry into his past. Saunders could not but grin when he thought of the Rossiters.

They would be sailing back to Australia once they had seen their daughter wedded to the gentlemanly Englishman who had been so kind and useful to them during their visit to the old country. They were in Paris now, buying Mary's trousseau, and he was to join them there for a little holiday – at their expense, of course.

Once the wedding was over they would not trouble him, but Maggie would – Maggie with her prison record as an expert sneak thief and pickpocket and, what was worse, her knowledge of his prison record.

It had been all that he could do to keep her in the background while he was cultivating the acquaintance of the Rossiters. Already she had tried a little gentle blackmail. Decidedly, there was not room in his life for Maggie and Mary.

And so to Bank Holiday, the day on which Saunders was to sail to meet the Rossiters in Paris, the day which he had decided on as Maggie's last.

To all appearance, nothing could have been more innocent than the little jaunt to the seaside that he proposed, and with which Maggie, who had been pestering him for his company for some time, fell in so readily.

Nothing more innocent than the elderly family saloon in which they pottered in an endless string of other elderly family saloons along the road to the coast that morning. (Somewhere a family was wondering what had become of their saloon, which they had incautiously left unattended in the West End. It had fresh number plates now and a skilfully altered licence.)

Nothing more natural than that the drive should have ended on the downs overlooking the harbour where the Channel boat was making ready to sail. And if the couple in the car chose to recline on the back seat very close in each other's arms, well, could anything be more natural than that?

There was a sharp breeze blowing in from the sea across the top of the hill and the car was only one of dozens parked nearby occupied by other couples similarly employed.

A flight of jet aircraft screamed overhead. Under cover of the sound, Saunders slipped out of the car.

By the time that the heads and eyes of the throng of

holidaymakers had turned from following them, he was yards away from it, an inconspicuous unit in the mass, making his way down a cliff path towards the sea.

It had been extraordinarily easy, he told himself – so easy that he almost felt apologetic towards the girl who had allowed herself to be snuffed out with so little trouble.

She had guessed that this Bank Holiday outing was in the nature of a last farewell but surprisingly she had not made a scene.

It was the only respect in which things had not gone according to plan.

He had braced himself for a quarrel, but there had been none. The foul-mouthed little thief had been sweetness and forgiveness itself.

She had only asked for a last kiss. And what a kiss! Saunders' lips still tingled with it as he strode nonchalantly along.

Which of course had made things childishly simple. A commando training in unarmed combat qualified a man to do harder things than squeezing the life out of a girl already limp and helpless in one's arms.

It was simply a matter of remembering one's instructions about pressure points . . .

All the same, it was a pity. Maggie must have loved him after all. Mary would never learn to kiss like that. Perhaps he had been wrong and could have kept them both. For a moment Saunders wondered whether it had been right to murder Maggie.

Still keeping up his unhurried stroll, Saunders approached the harbour. He had worked to a careful timetable, and like everything else on this successful day, it fitted perfectly.

A boat train was just coming in. A flood of chattering tourists surged towards the Customs' Sheds. Saunders allowed himself to be caught up in the crowd and waited patiently as it formed into a queue.

Slowly now, step by step, they moved forward, jostling, laughing, humping one another with their suitcases and haversacks. Somewhere ahead a tired voice was chanting 'British passports this way! Have your passports ready, please!'

It was not until he had nearly reached the barrier that Saunders felt in his breast pocket – felt once, twice and yet again in desperate unbelief. Then he fell out of the queue and began to go through all the pockets in his suit, in vain.

He tore open the little bag that he carried and found nothing there but his things for a night or two away from home.

'Have your passport ready, please!' the voice repeated just over his head. 'British passports this way!'

A long time after, it seemed to Saunders, another voice close by him said, 'Lost your passport, sir? That's a bit of bad luck. Perhaps you had your pocket picked? It happens here sometimes, you know.'

Saunders nodded dumbly. He could still feel Maggie's arms as they went tenderly around him in that last close embrace.

'Afraid you can't go on board without a passport,' the voice went on. 'Spoiled your holiday, I'm afraid. But I shouldn't worry too much, sir, just give the particulars in at the office. The police will find it all right.'

And sure enough, they did.

Cyril Hare

Questions

1 What do you find about Maggie's background and 'occupation'?
2 Why was it so easy to persuade Maggie to go for a day out to the seaside?
3 How did the murderer expect Maggie to behave when she knew the trip was a 'farewell'?
4 How did she actually behave?
5 Why did Maggie ask for a last kiss? What does this show about her character?
6 How had Maggie caused the ending of the story to be different from the one planned by Saunders?

Essay work

Write a story with one of these titles. Make sure that the events of the story happen because of the characters of the people involved. **Use the skills** that you have learned from *The Old Flame*.

The Gambler
The Manager
The Dancer
The Long Distance Lorry Driver
The Trainer

Using character in playwriting

Characters are very important in playwriting. It is through them that the story is told.
A person's character is shown in the following ways:
— what the character does;
— what the character says;
— what others say about him or her.

You need to set your script out properly. Look at the following extract.

That's a lovely fresh herring

(They all sit down to tea: Rafe is at the head of the table, Florence left of him, and Harold on his right. Wilfred sits on Harold's right, and Daisy below Harold. Hilda is down left of Florence, where she is conspicuous to the audience.)

> Describe
> the scene
> here

> Do not use
> speech marks

RAFE What was that, Mother?
DAISY A little something I borrowed off our Florence.
RAFE (quoting) 'Neither a borrower nor a lender be . . .'
HAROLD Hey, Wilf, pass the tartar sauce.
WILFRED The what?
FLORENCE Sauce tartare. (She picks it up.) Here you are.
HAROLD Ta ta. 'For loan oft loses both itself and friend.' Do you fancy some, Dad?

> Put each
> character's
> speech on
> a new line.

> Give advice to the
> actor on what
> to do here.

79

> The writer shows clearly the characters of the members of the family in the rest of the scene. Read it carefully and answer the questions.

RAFE	I prefer the natural taste of the herring.
HAROLD	I find this sauce quite piquant. How much a jar is it, Mum?
DAISY	I don't know – oh, one and ninepence. I knew there was something I didn't write down. (*She starts to rise, then sits.*) I'll do it later.

(*Rafe looks at her.*)

HAROLD	What about you, Florence?
FLORENCE	I'll give it a miss. These taste lovely as they are.
HILDA	I say, Mum, I really don't fancy my herring – if you don't mind.
DAISY	No, of course not, love! What would you like instead? I've got some nice fresh eggs.
HAROLD	Aye, with some streaky rashers.
HILDA	No, just an egg.
HAROLD	Sunny side up?
HILDA	Done on both sides. But wait till you've finished, Mum.
DAISY	It's all right, love – won't take me a minute. (*Rising*) You must be ready for it after a day's work ...

(*They think they have got away with it, but Rafe quietly beckons Daisy to sit.*)

RAFE	Hold on a minute, Mother. (*To Hilda*) Is there something wrong with your herring?
HILDA	No, nothing wrong with it – only I don't feel like it.
RAFE	That's a lovely fresh herring, it's been done in best butter, and yet you have the nerve to sit there and say you don't feel like it.
HILDA	What else can I say if I don't?
RAFE	You can eat it and say nothing.
HAROLD	Well, that's asking a bit much, Dad!
HILDA	I'll just go and fry myself an egg, Mum.
RAFE	No you won't.
HILDA	Why not?
RAFE	Because this is a home, not a cafeteria.
HILDA	I'm entitled to some choice over what I have for my tea – I'm bringing my share of money into the home.

RAFE You don't think I thought less of you over all the years you never brought a ha'penny? I'd as soon see the smiling face you had in them days than you were bringing twenty pounds a week home today.

WILFRED Here, Dad, to save any bother, I'll eat our Hilda's herring.

RAFE You'll do nothing of the sort. You get on with your own tea.

DAISY (*not put out*) Dad – it wouldn't take a second to fry an egg.

RAFE There's no fried eggs coming on the scene.

HILDA Then there's no point in my waiting here. (Rising) Excuse me, everybody – I'll just go upstairs . . .

RAFE (*quietly*) No you won't. Sit down.

HILDA What?

RAFE I said sit down.

(*Hilda is undecided. Daisy gives her a pleading look.*)

Pigs leave their troughs when it suits – but not civilised human beings.

(*Wilfred gives Hilda a look of sympathetic support, Florence gives her a reproving glance. Harold continues to eat with an air of detached interest about the outcome. Daisy does not want any trouble but gives Hilda a comforting, motherly look.*)

DAISY Dad – I'll just . . .

(*Rafe remains oddly above it all, continuing to eat naturally as he talks. Hilda catches Daisy's look and sits down, but away from the table.*)

RAFE No you won't, Mother. They were never spoilt when young – it 'ud be a pity to start now. One day, young woman, you may realise what words like home and family mean. A man and woman marry, they have children, feed and tend 'em, work for 'em, guide, aye an' love 'em.

HILDA Just as they ought.

RAFE Aye, I agree – as they ought. Over the years they try to make a home for those children, not just a furnished place to live in, but a home, mark you, with some culture. But do those children thank you? Well, perhaps some do – mostly they don't. They take you an' your home for granted. Well, there's nobody taking me for granted.

HILDA I don't see why I should eat that herring if I don't want it . . .

RAFE (*detached*) Then I'll tell you one reason why – as comes to

mind at the moment. Pass me the bread, Florence, please.
Have you ever heard of the Hunger Marchers?

(*Florence passes the bread. Rafe takes a piece.*)

DAISY   Dad – calm yourself.

RAFE   I can't stand the way young people are today – all for themselves, and all for the present, as though the past didn't
exist.

DAISY   (*Always achieving a balance of sympathy*) More tea Dad?

RAFE   No thank you, Mother – not just now. (*Rising*) But there is
one thing you can do for me – have that herring of our
Hilda's safely put on one side – and you serve it to her, and
nothing else, at every meal – until she eats it! I'm having no
more sloppy living under my roof. (*He picks up his jacket.*)

HILDA   I won't eat it . . .

RAFE   We'll see – because you'll eat nothing at my table until you
have. (*He picks up his collar and tie.*)

HILDA   I won't touch it! Not if it's there till kingdom come!

RAFE   Right, we'll see the outcome. I'll go and get ready for my
union meeting. If you get the better of me you'll be the first
in this house who has. Mother, I'm relying on you over that
herring.

DAISY   I'll get it out of the way at once, Dad.

(*Rafe goes out. Daisy has seen quarrels come and go and doesn't take them
too seriously. She gives Hilda a pat, then goes to the kitchen with the herring.*)

HAROLD   (*to Hilda*) Don't worry – they'll be comin' to take him away
in the yellow cab very soon, the way he's going on. He's
obsessed.

from Spring and Port Wine by Bill Naughton

Questions

1   What do you find about Rafe's, Daisy's and Hilda's characters in
this extract?

To help you organise your ideas, draw up some columns like
those which follow.

A What he says	Character
What was that, Mother? No you won't.	Inquisitive Domineering

B What he does	Character

C What others say about him	Character

2   In the correct column, write down something that Rafe says, does, or is said about him. In the second column, write down a word which describes what is being shown about his character. An example has been done for you.

3   Set out your ideas on Hilda and Daisy in the same way.

4   Using the information you have collected, write a paragraph on each of these characters explaining what sort of people they are.

Practice work   Choose another incident which would cause an upset in a family. Write a scene about the argument. Show the characters of the people involved, through what they say and do, and through what is said about them.

The characters in a play make the plot in the same way as they do in a story. At the beginning you need to make clear the following points.
Who are the characters?
Where is the play set?
When does it take place?
What is the plot?

First Day at Work

(The play takes place in a small Midlands town. The time is the present.

Scene One Just before 9.00 am at Carlton's, a large firm. During the scene the action moves between two areas, an office used by a group of typists, and Mr Neale's personal office, which is smaller, but more luxurious. If possible, both should be visible all the time, and the movement between the two should be managed through lighting, as smoothly and quickly as possible.

In the typists' office, Mrs Prentiss is busy, tidying papers efficiently. Alison comes in and hangs up her coat.)

ALISON	Morning Mrs P.
MRS P	Hello, Alison. Have a nice weekend?
ALISON	Oh yes. Went to a great concert on Saturday.
MRS P	Not my sort of concert, I suppose.
ALISON	It might be. You don't know till you try.
MRS P	I don't think so.

(*Shelley comes in, a bit breathless.*)

SHELLEY	Morning, Alison. Morning, Mrs Prentiss.
MRS P	Good morning.
ALISON	Hi, Shelley. Have a good time?
SHELLEY	Too good. I'd rather have stayed in bed than clock in here.
MRS P	Well, it's Monday morning and you can't change that.
SHELLEY	I wouldn't mind trying.
MRS P	Anything to get out of work.
ALISON	Now, now, Mrs P, we haven't started yet.

(*Clare looks in, a bit nervously.*)

MRS P	Can I help you?
CLARE	I'm Clare Holden. I'm starting here today.
MRS P	Come in, love. Have you seen Mr Neale?
CLARE	Not today. I saw him when I came for my interview. He said to come to the third floor and ask for Mrs Prentiss.
MRS P	That's me.

SHELLEY	You're going to work here, then?
CLARE	Well I'd like to.
SHELLEY	Are you in the union?
MRS P	Give her a chance, she's hardly got here.
SHELLEY	I'm giving her a chance – a chance to join.
MRS P	Clare's only on a month's trial to start with. There'll be time enough for joining the union if she's given a permanent job. Have you done typing and shorthand?
CLARE	Yes, but only at college. This is my first job.
SHELLEY	Well, you've chosen a good place to start. Mrs P'll look after you, so long as you work twenty four hours a day and don't stop to blow your nose.
MRS P	That's quite enough of that.
SHELLEY	All right, Mrs P, you know I'm joking.
MRS P	I'm never sure when you're serious, that's the trouble.
ALISON	You've been before, though, to your interview?
CLARE	Yes, with Mr Neale. He seemed very nice.
SHELLEY	Oh, Neale's all right. It's Morley you've got to watch.
MRS P	Don't be rude about Mr Morley. He works very hard.
SHELLEY	He works us hard, I know that. I'm not sure why they moved him in above Neale, but I know who I'd rather have.

(*Neale comes in cheerily.*)

NEALE	Good morning, Mrs Prentiss. Good morning girls. Shelley, could I have a word in my office in a minute? Oh yes, . . . Clare Holden, isn't it?
CLARE	Yes, that's right.
NEALE	You found your way here all right, then?
CLARE	Yes, thank you.
NEALE	Well, Mrs Prentiss will take care of any problems. Just find your way around, and do your best. We'll give you a month and see how you go, all right?
CLARE	Yes. Thank you, Mr Neale.
NEALE	Right, I'll see you in a minute, then? (*Goes*)
SHELLEY	Righto, Mr Neale. (*Looks in her bag.*) Here, Clare, there's a union card. You can leave joining till you've got a permanent job if you like, but this'll tell you what it's about. I'll tell you about meetings over lunch. Must dash. (*Goes out.*)
CLARE	(*a bit dazed*) Oh . . . er . . . right.

ALISON	There you are. It's as easy as that. Don't blink or you'll find you're a paid-up member.
MRS P	I don't know why they bother.
CLARE	I don't really know anything about it . . .
ALISON	Don't worry. Just leave it to Shelley. She's a good organis-er, and she'll let you know what's happening.
MRS P	All in good time, she will. First of all we'll get some work done – that is what we're here for, after all. Now, Clare, I'd like you to file these letters over here, clients in alphabetical order of surnames, most recent correspond-ence at the front of the file, and then there's some of Mr Neale's correspondence . . .

(The scene is in Mr Neale's office, where Mr Morley is in the middle of a brief visit.)

MORLEY	So it looks as though there'll have to be a definite cut back on staffing.
NEALE	Finding people to retire early, you mean. That sort of thing.
MORLEY	Well, I suppose that might help to begin with, but I'm look-ing for something rather more far-reaching.

from *See How You Go* by Paul Francis

Questions

1 What do you find out about the main characters in the play?
2 What information are you given about the place where it is set? Draw a sketch of the setting to help you with your explanation.
3 What are you told about time in the play? (time of day; time of year; past, present or future)
4 Look carefully at what the characters say, and then explain what ideas you have about the way the plot will develop in each play.

Picture   Use the picture to write a suitable first scene of a playscript.

Essay work   Here are some essay questions for you to choose from. You need to **use the skills** you have learned so far, to describe the following people. A full description of the characters will include details about their appearance, actions, mannerisms and the way they speak. If you are writing a play or a story use character to make the plot.

1   **The Stranger** – write about a time when you saw someone who you did not know, but who stood out from the crowd and interested you for some reason. Describe the person showing what impression of his or her character you were given.

2   Describe two people who are **close friends**. Show what it is about their characters which makes them get on well together.

3   I had arrived early in the morning and soon discovered that I was thrown amid the oddest collection of persons I had ever encountered.

Continue by describing each of the people in turn, showing why it was an 'odd collection of persons'.

4   When Mr Montgomery walked into the room we all went silent.

Continue by telling Mr Montgomery's story, showing the type of person he must be.

5   Mrs Jones lived alone in a small house at the end of our street. I was sure she was the oldest woman in the world.

Describe the character of this solitary old lady, and tell her story.

6   Write a play with one of these titles.

Monday Morning
The Nosy Neighbour
A Helping Hand
Condemned
It's Lovely to See You

4 Personal writing

Personal writing is when you write about yourself. When you describe something you did in detail, describe how you felt as well as
what happened. You can also describe people you know and why
you remember them.

Giving the facts

The simplest way to write about yourself or your experiences is to give the facts as you remember them. You need to give plenty of detail to make sure that what you say is clear and interesting. Read the following account of a motorbike ride written by a sixteen year old girl.

Ton-up!

The time was 7.30. Black leather jackets with studs and badges caught the gleam from the street lights. The rockers were gathering together for a ton-up! No crash helmets worn, they mounted their bikes. My boyfriend, Pete, had a 650 Norton. With his eyes gleaming, his face set with determination, he gave the bike a kick. With a roar the machine started, Pete revving it up so that people got out of the way.

I climbed onto the back and put my hands behind me. (You never hold on.) Then we were away! He lay across the red tank, head held low, the chrome wheels shining in the night. You feel so big, so daring: people shout and accuse you of being mad and not considering others on the road.

But you don't care; you stick your two fingers back at them! The speedometer goes past the 100 going down Box Hill. You roar in and out, weaving your way through the string of traffic. Then you overtake when you know full well a car or lorry is approaching the other way. It comes closer, closer, lights flashing to tell you to get in. As a pillion passenger you shut your eyes and pray hard. You feel the bike swerve. When you open your eyes again everything is calm and the roar of the engine speeds on down the hill. When you're on a bike no one else matters. You are in a world of your own.

The bike begins to drop speed and slow down. Finally it stops. Then the gang, on their bikes, gather to a stop outside the coffee bar. You get off, your eyes running, stinging with the wind that blew against you on the bike. You go in the coffee bar, have a coke, and plan when next to have another ton-up. Perhaps next time you won't be so lucky. There may be accidents or police screwing you for speed. But you do it just for kicks! It's your unlucky number if you never return from a ton-up!

Questions

1 What details does the girl give of the scene before the ride?
2 What facts does she give about the ride?
3 What information does she give about what she does and how she feels after the motorbike ride?
4 What does she mean by 'It's your unlucky number if you never return from a ton-up!'? What does this tell you about her attitude?
5 The girl describes the experience in a very factual way. What other information could she have given? Refer to specific points in her account when she could have given it.

Practice work
Picture

Write about something that has happened to you suggested by either the pictures on page 92 or the titles. Give the facts and details in a lively way.

A night at the youth club
The end of term

Describing emotion

When you are writing about yourself describe your emotions. To do this think about a situation which made you sad, happy, afraid, embarrassed etc. Make the emotion **clear** to the reader. Adjectives and comparisons will help you to do this well. The following extracts describe very different emotions.

The Policeman

How the humiliations of one's youth remain with one. To this day I am crippled with embarrassment whenever I confront a policeman, because of my experiences at eight years old.

My 'gang' were sports-mad and highly intrepid and would do anything to prove what I thought was their manhood. I was considerably younger than they were, and therefore had a great inferiority complex. I was not entirely 'accepted' by them and I felt that I had always to be doing something that proved my own worthiness in their eyes. Unfortunately my response to policemen did not help matters, for, quite frankly, I was scared of them. Apple-stealing ventures, raids on rival gangs, avoiding paying bus fares, swinging from the backs of moving lorries or outrageous tricks on bicycles were things in which I had to partake or bring upon myself a storm of ridicule. I did so with fear and trembling of the men in blue.

Now there was one thing that the boys would never do and that was steal the pears of Mr Tucker who lived on the corner of Brecon Road and Limegrove Avenue. They looked delicious every year. In fact, their apparent succulence increased with each succeeding autumn. But not one of the gang would dare touch them.

And yet they were easy to get at, situated in the corner of the garden and actually overhanging the road. The garden was surrounded by a not too difficult fence to climb – we had scaled many more difficult stockades at the Alamo or Fort Worth – and hoards of pears could easily be reached. Mrs Wright's gooseberry fence or Mr Tapp's orchard wall had proved much more difficult, but no one would consider

an attack on Mr Tucker's pear tree. Why, we could not quite say. Mr Tucker was a formidable man who would not hesitate to clout one of us, and he had a fearsome Alsatian dog who roamed the garden freely; but there was more to him than this. He was a solitary man; he never spoke to his neighbours; he was not a friend of our parents; nor was he married. His house was darkly painted and heavily curtained, and we had never seen it entered by a single soul. There was something forbidding about Mr Tucker that nobody could quite pinpoint but would dare defy.

One day the 'gang' had been particularly harsh on me for refusing to join them in running in front of an express train as it tore down towards Meadow Hill Station. They, being older than I was, could run faster so that by the time I came to run across the line the iron monster was almost upon me. Naturally I was frightened out of my wits but they did not see it this way. To them I was just a little coward barely worthy of being carried along. I did not mind being the baby of the 'gang' but I did want to be accepted by it so their taunts, their ridiculing, their mockery hurt me very much and I just had to prove that I was not the coward that they thought I was.

We stood at the corner of Brecon and Limegrove. It was a rich autumn day and Mr Tucker's pears imposed themselves upon us against the vivid blue, sleek sky. Between our jiblings* we looked at them enviously.

'Couldn't you go on one?' said Bill jealously.

'Not 'alf,' said Terry, 'if I 'ad the guts!'

I cannot think why I said it. In fact, I do not really remember saying it all.

'I'll get some!' I blurted out. They all looked at me in amazement.

'You!' exclaimed Preb. 'You wouldn't even smoke a Woodbine!'

'All right!' I said, sticking stubbornly to my offer but secretly already regretting it. 'You see!'

And nonchalantly I strolled over to the fence and surveyed it for a foothold. I found one and put my foot in it.

* teasing, complaining

My heart was nearly exploding in my breast, and I was bursting for a pee as I looked around to see if anyone was coming. The coast was clear, but I could not back out now because I knew the 'gang' were watching me from behind front gates and garden fences.

I got a foothold and pulled myself to the top of the fence. It was easier than I had thought, and I could not even see old Tucker's Alsatian. I eased my way along the fence inch by inch until I was immediately beneath the tree. Within reach were a host of the largest and most luscious pears that I had ever seen. I stopped to look at them for a moment – they appeared so harmonious against the cool yellow of the turning leaves and the filmy azure sky that to pick them seemed a barbarous act. However, I could wait no longer. Old Tucker might appear at any moment.

I reached my arm up and felt the smooth roundness of a saffron coloured pear fill my hand. Just as I was about to pull it from its bedding I suddenly felt a large hand grip the seat of my pants. I let go of the pear and looked down. There standing immediately beneath me with an outstretched navy blue arm reaching for my bottom was a tall policeman. I was so scared and inert that the only thing I could do was let my already bursting bladder explode. It poured from my short trousers and ran like a stream down the policeman's sleeve. He must have been soaked but he did not flinch. He just lifted me down from the fence with his dripping arm and said sternly:

'What do you think you're doing?' as though nothing extraordinary had happened.

The sound of his voice brought me back to reality and I futilely tugged against his powerful arm in an attempt to run away. I felt sure that this was the end for me. However, all the policeman said was:

'Don't ever let me catch you doing that again or you'll be for the high jump, my son. Now run off home quickly and get cleaned up.'

I think that if the truth were known he was more anxious than I was to run off home and get cleaned up because he hopped on his bicycle quickly enough and pedalled off. But

I wasted no time. I burst into tears and tore home like a frightened rabbit, crying all the way up Brecon Road.

Naturally after that, I was the laughing stock of the whole 'gang', and I did not even have any fruit to show for it. In fact, the news spread to the whole district and I was ridiculed about the incident for the rest of my days there. I never got over the humiliation – and as if to pour salt into an already grievous wound, the next time that I saw that policeman, I noticed that he had been promoted to sergeant!

from *The Policeman* by Alan Crang

Questions

1   Why was the writer not accepted by the gang? What effect did this have on him?

2   What was the writer's attitude to the policeman? Which words tell you this?

3   How did the gang treat the writer when he would not do their 'dares'? Which words tell you? How did the writer feel?

4   How did he pretend he felt after he offered to steal the pears? Which words or expressions tell you this?

5   How did he really feel? How do you know?

6   What does the comparison 'I tore home like a frightened rabbit' tell you about how the writer felt after he had been caught? How did the other boys treat him?

7   What hurt him most about the whole incident? Why?

8   What seems to be the writer's attitude to this experience as he looks back.

In the next extract, Frank Norman describes an incident from his childhood spent in Dr Barnardo's Homes. The story of his part in the second eleven football match would be very funny but for what happened afterwards.

The Football Match

At the end of the first half the visitors were two goals up, one of their own and one of mine. During the break I kept well out of harm's way at the other end of the field.

At the commencement of the second half, the captain of our side ordered me in no uncertain terms to keep well out of the way and not to touch the ball, unless there was absolutely no other alternative. I willingly complied with his wishes and confined myself to parts of the field where the ball was not. Within fifteen minutes the Home side had scored two goals; their blood was up and they played like tigers – several fouls were incurred. But the referee (a member of the staff) turned a blind eye to them. The visitors retaliated but were unable to score a third goal. I have to own that the Barnardo Boys put on a fine show, especially as they were playing with one man short, for I was contributing nothing whatever to their success.

Several minutes before the final whistle I stood minding my own business in the penalty area of our goal when suddenly I turned to see the ball cannonading in my direction, with all the members of both sides charging after it. Pedro had often told me of the bullfights of his home land, and at that moment I knew exactly how a torero must feel when an enraged bull bears down on him. They were all yelling at the tops of their voices and I would have fled if I had not been riveted to the spot through fear. A member of the opposing side gave the ball a pulverising kick straight at my face. I put up my hands to protect myself and the ball bounced off them, the force of the kick knocking me to the ground. 'Hand ball!' they yelled in unison. The referee blew his brains out on the whistle and awarded a penalty kick to the villagers. The boys jeered at me and threatened my life as the captain of the other side placed the ball on the penalty spot and thundered the ball into the net. Our goalie had not the slightest chance of saving it for the shot was true and as straight as an arrow.

The whistle blew, indicating the end of the game and perhaps the end of my life. My head bowed in shame, I ambled along behind my fellows to the showers; no one spoke to me as we entered the washhouse, but the atmosphere was electric and I knew that I was doomed. As we took off our football togs two of them came over to me and became insulting. I tried to explain to them that I had been shanghaied into the game, but although they were well aware of that it seemed to make no difference. Without warning one of them took a swing at me, which caught me on the side of the head and sent me sprawling on the floor. Painfully I staggered to my feet hoping that that was going to be the end to it, but no such luck, the great oaf struck me again and once more I hit the deck. Another of the boys, completely unable to contain himself, pounced on top of me and began to pummel my body. Crouching, I covered my face with my hands as best I could but still suffered considerable damage. 'Okay that's enough,' said the referee who must have been present throughout the whole of the proceedings, but had not bothered to intervene. The boy stopped hitting me and with a black eye, split lip and multiple bruises I staggered to my feet and wandered quietly away by myself without uttering another word. At tea that evening the assembled boys glanced at me askance but no one said a word.

That evening Pedro tried to comfort me, but I was inconsolable so after a time he gave it up as a bad job and left me alone. As I lay on my bed staring at the ceiling, my eyes blinded with tears, I resolved to escape from this inhuman hell-hole. But how and where would I go? I had no money and knew absolutely no one outside the Home, but I did not care, I would abscond and leave the rest to destiny.

from *Banana Boy* by Frank Norman

Questions

1 What was the first thing the writer had done which made the boys angry? How did they treat him?
2 How did the writer feel when the ball came towards him? Which words tell you?
3 How did the boys treat the writer when he gave away the penalty?
4 How did he feel as he entered the changing rooms? How do you know?
5 Which words show the viciousness of the boys' attack?
6 How do you think he felt when he says he 'wandered away quietly by myself without uttering another word'?
7 How did the writer feel as he lay in bed? Which words tell you this?
8 What do you think the writer's attitude is to the experience as he looks back?

Practice work

Draw up columns like those below.

Emotion	Adjectives	Comparisons
Anger	angry, furious, violent, aggressive	As furious as a hissing cat; as violent as an erupting volcano

In the first column, put the word anger. In the second column, write as many adjectives as you can which show anger. Some are done for you. In the third column, write some comparisons which could be used to show anger. Remember to make your comparisons original. Now do the same for each of the following emotions: **love, hate, happiness, fear, sadness**.

Choose one of the emotions and write about a time you experienced it. Describe what happened and how you felt.

Writing about experiences

When you write about an experience, show what made that experience important or special. It may be the first time you have done something or it may have changed your life in some way. You can describe the experience in a **factual** way, you can make it **humorous** or you can make the reader feel **sympathetic** towards you.

> The following extracts deal with young love. In the first one, Michael Baldwin describes his first kiss.

How should I ever?

Well. I'd danced with someone. Had she seen me dancing? I went to find her to ask her to dance with me. She was nowhere in the Village Hall. Nor was Tony.

She was waiting outside.

'What you doing out here?' I asked.

'Waiting,' she said.

Someone was coming, very slowly, out of the men's lavatory behind her. It was Tony. Fancy being able to tell her without blushing that he wanted to go in there! I wondered what he'd said to her.

'Leaving?' I asked.

'Just walking home with Anne,' he said. He even knew her name.

'Thanks,' I said. 'But I've told you about this.' And I pushed his chest hard.

He went to hit me, and as he was going to hit me I thought: he'll hurt me, he's in a fury, he'll come for me in a rage and my fists won't stop him. I always did badly if people lost their temper. But then he didn't hit me. There were tears in his eyes, and I sneered at him. But my chest was knocking, I shuddered with it, to tell me how frightened I'd been.

I daren't say anything to him in case he got in that rage again, and anyway my mouth tasted empty, there was nothing in it to say. I just turned and took hold of her by the arm. 'Do you mind?' she said, which was all girls did say when you said or did anything they didn't like. But she came with me. My mouth tasted better, and as we walked on and he stood there I noticed there was moonlight still on the hedges.

'Nice, old Tony,' I said. 'Just a kid, though.'

'Mum's expecting him for cocoa,' she said.

I couldn't say anything for a bit. It wasn't that he'd been creeping behind me and dancing with her and finding out her name and putting his hand up and down her back – I was going to kill him for that on the bus in the morning. It was that he'd been able to find this secret with her, just the way they looked at one another – I could tell there was something between boys and girls that I was being left out of. We walked on together. She kept jerking away from me. I knew my hand was hurting her arm, but I daren't let her go.

I tried to start her talking.

'I like cocoa,' I said.

'I hate it,' she said. 'Filthy muck.'

'Why drink it?' I asked.

'Mummy says.'

'Sounds nice, your mum.'

'I hate her.'

'Make much money out of farming, your dad?'

'You want to marry me or something?'

'I'm only twelve,' I said. It sounded daft once I'd said it, especially since she was thirteen.

She laughed at me. 'Well, you can't anyway. Daddy says I've got to marry someone rich enough to pay off his mortgage, and Mummy says it ought to be someone with the same initials as me – to save changing my laundry labels.' We were at her front gate now, I noticed. 'And that's not you,' she said.

Anthony, Anne. Tony's winning already, I thought. I daren't ask her what her surname was. That might be Tony's luck as well.

She pulled away from me, and pushed open the big gate at one end. But I still had her arm, and tugged her back towards me, the gate already between us, and its end post jarring my elbow. All girls want it, Robert had said, so I held on tightly, and the bars of the gate crunched against me and the bottom rung gave me a quick sick knock on the shin as she turned her face all indifferently up to me – I should have remembered the way that gate swung. The moon in her eyes made them laugh, whatever she was feeling, and I kissed her.

'Ouch!' she said.

I'd done it too quickly. I'd tried to kiss her cheek and somehow I'd hurt her.

'Thanks for the bite,' she said, as if my mouth had been open or something.

'Sorry,' I said, and I let go of her.

Or perhaps my mouth hadn't been open, perhaps it was a good kiss, a very good kiss, like it was for me, only it was too late now. She was giggling away in the darkness, then knocking at her front door, and how should I ever know?

'Here,' I whispered.

But the door opened and I turned and ran.

Next day, after school, I looked for my friend, not Tony, my town friend, who was better than Tony. Besides, I hadn't hit Tony as hard as I wanted; he'd start hitting back, and once or twice he'd hurt me.

When I found him, he was up at the cycle shed.

'Something bothering you?' he said.

'Am I good looking?' I asked.

He looked at me for a long time. He was very shy and quiet and that was why he was my friend.

'I don't know,' he said. 'Your eyebrows meet in the middle.'

'I can't help it,' I said. I was nearly in tears.

'No. I mean – my eyebrows meet too.'

So they did.

He was embarrassed about something. 'And I read, in my mother's magazines, that men whose eyebrows meet in the middle are irresistible to women.'

I remembered the looks girls gave him at parties.

But my eyebrows meet as well.

'Can I ask you a favour?' I asked.

'What?'

'I want to kiss you.'

He couldn't believe he'd heard properly. I could see that.

'I just want to kiss you on the cheek and I want you to tell me if it hurts, that's all.'

'Don't be silly,' he said.

'Please.'

'I've got to be going, anyway.'

He got up and put his cycle-clips on and then swung his leg over his bike. I'd missed my bus now, waiting for him and anyway I didn't want to catch that one again.

'So long,' he said.

'So long,' I said.

He waited.

'Just once,' I said. 'I just want to know if it hurts your cheek.'

'Don't be silly.' He pushed the pedal noisily, and cycled away, not sitting in his saddle. 'You'll have to find someone else.'

But if I couldn't ask him, who could I ask, ever?

from *Sebastian and Other Voices* by Michael Baldwin

Questions

1 How do you know the writer has not been out with any girls before?

2 How does he make his description of his first kiss amusing?

3 What worries does he have about his relationship with girls?

4 How does he try to find the answer to his problems and how does he make it amusing?

5 How do you feel about the writer when he says at the end 'But if I couldn't ask him, who could I ask, ever?'?

In this extract, Leslie Thomas describes taking a girl to the theatre. 'Dickies' is the name for the Dr Barnardo's Home where he spent his childhood. Surbiton, where the girl lives, is a wealthy area in Surrey. The 'gods' are the cheapest seats at the very top of the theatre.

Young Love

My girl was waiting, a trifle impatiently because she was like that. But she looked nice with her dark hair and her red coat and her high-heeled shoes. As I went to buy the tickets I felt as big and confident as though I came from Surbiton too. She made a small pouting face when I bought two tickets for the remotest gods, and she grumbled all the way up the stairs, pointing out that at this rate we would never have time for a drink before the concert began.

Everything inside me froze when I heard her say this. Frantically I began counting the coins in my pocket so that I could buy her drinks. Fool! Why hadn't I realised that? Of course she would want drinks. You couldn't just take a woman to a concert and expect her to be satisfied with that. You had to think of other things and other expenses. Like drinks.

Every step up to the gallery was a stony misery. I delayed her for a while by pretending to have to do up my shoelaces, and to my wild relief this took up an essential minute, for when we got to our seats by the rail and the awful chasm, the orchestra was just beginning to tune.

We were a long way up, so far that you could count the bald heads in the audience and the orchestra with ease. We peered over the cliff as the conductor arrived, and was immediately partially obscured by a small skein of smoke which wriggled across just below us.

'The last time I came, when I was with Paul,' she said with arch sweetness, 'we sat down there.' She leaned over and pointed with her thin Surbiton finger to the fifth row of the stalls, distant, indistinct, with toy people sitting in them.

'You get a better view up here,' I said sadly but stubbornly, and she replied something that I did not catch because the music began.

I leaned on the rail and, as ever, became lost in the splendid and lovely sounds that sometimes drifted, sometimes roared, from below. She sat upright emitting little sniffling noises, and interrupting my dream by asking me if I would mind lighting her cigarette.

There was quite a bit of smoke coming up from below and she fanned herself irritably with the programme that I had purchased for a precious shilling. She did not read it, she just fanned her sharp little face with it.

I had just mentally placed the soloist in the piano concerto on the right hand of God, when she said quite loudly that she thought he sounded tinny, and when she came with Paul so-and-so was playing and he was bliss.

At the interval we sat fidgeting for a while before, as I had feared, she suggested that we went and had a drink. There was no escape now, no shoelace tying, no procrastination of any kind, for she was making smart little steps towards the bar.

Never in my life had I been in a bar of any sort. I knew from the films that you used various phrases to ask people what they would like to drink, and with a small satisfaction I remembered one from a picture we had seen at Dickies the previous Saturday.

'What's your poison?' I said, moving close to her and looking into her dark Surbiton eyes.

She giggled disconcertingly and said firmly: 'Gin and ton for me.'

I went to jelly. Gin and ton! Whatever it was, it sounded as though it cost quids. I would have to tell her, I just would, there was no going on with this.

But she smiled like sunshine before I could confess and she said: 'We'd better hurry, darling.'

Darling! This angel, with her high-heeled shoes and her gin and ton, had called me darling! Me with my yellow tie and my suit that not so long before I had worn for running away.

The endearment caught me up in a cloud and I staggered

towards the bar. She was in love with me then. Girls didn't call you darling unless they were in love with you. All the time she had been hiding it, and doing it very well too.

And she called me that – and other people were standing around and they must have heard her saying it too. When people were in love in films they said that, but I did not think she would call me it. Darling!

I wondered if the woman at the bar had heard her. 'Gin and ton please, darling,' I said.

'Not so much lip!' she replied smartly, and I realised what I had said. 'Gin and tonic is it, and what else?'

My feet, both of them were on the ground again now. 'Nothing else, thanks,' I whispered. 'I'm not drinking. How much is it?'

'You don't look old enough for a start,' she said pouring the gin anyway. 'That will be one and eight.'

I returned to the girl bearing the gin and tonic as though it were a love potion. 'Gin and ton,' I said idly.

'Good,' she sniffed. 'Aren't you going to have something?'

'I'm on the wagon,' I said, feeling immediately pleased that the phrase tripped off so lithely. 'Football training, you know. We're not allowed to drink.'

'How boring,' she said, pouring the remainder of my one and eightpence down her red throat. 'Let's get back to this awful concert. Really, when I came with Paul . . .'

All the second half I crouched over the rail like a gargoyle, laden with despair now because I had realised that I did not have enough money to pay for our return fares. The music came up to mock me and she sniffed audibly on the quiet passages, while I wondered what sort of a sensation I would cause by throwing myself into the chasm before me.

I had no serious intention of doing this, although I felt full enough of woe. The only way out of the mess, I decided, short of telling her that I came from Dickies, was to take her to Waterloo Station, buy her ticket and remember a sudden appointment on the other side of London.

The picture became composed in my mind and I became

quite pleased with it. I would take her to the platform, kiss her softly but quickly, and like some strange agent or adventurer, would vanish into the crowd. She would sit on the train to Surbiton wondering about this mysterious man with whom she had become involved – well, she did call me 'darling', didn't she? – and I would try and walk home.

But I did not have even the satisfaction of this gallantry. We arrived at Waterloo and she produced a season ticket and said I need not bother to pay her fare. At least it saved me the walk. We sat stiffly, politely, on the train all the way to Surbiton in the rain. She had not called me darling again and I was feeling wretched. At Surbiton Station she fenced with the idea of getting a taxi but like a glowing, fat angel on wheels a trolleybus flew around the corner and we boarded that instead.

We sat on top and presently she rose, announced that this was her stop, and held out a white limp hand that my heart must have resembled at that moment.

''Bye,' she said. 'Nice evening. See you.'

Then she had gone, jolting down the stairs, and out on to the rainy pavement, leaving me wrung out, disappointed, and cursing Dickies and the fate that made me belong to it. If I had taken her in the stalls like Paul, whoever he was, and given her plenty of gin and tons, and got a taxi from the station, it would have been different. We would have madly embraced in the taxi and then . . . oh hell, wasn't it murder with women!

from *This Time Next Week* by Leslie Thomas

Questions

1 How did taking the girl out make the writer feel?
2 What was the first problem he met and what did he do about it?
3 What does the girl feel about where they sit? How does the writer make the picture of them amusing?
4 What happens when the writer goes to the bar? Pick out some examples where he makes fun of himself.
5 How does the writer imagine himself saying goodnight to the girl?
6 What actually happens? How does it make you feel towards the writer?
7 How does the writer feel after the whole experience?
   How do you think he feels now as an adult about what happened? Give some examples of the way he tells the story to back up your view.

Practice work   Write about your first love or first date. Show why it was special to you. Describe whether it was a humorous or sad occasion.

Essay work   **Use the skills** you have learned in this chapter to answer the following.

1   Take the practice work pieces you have already done in this chapter and put them together to form your *Autobiography*. Write an introduction and a conclusion and illustrate your work.

2   A magazine publishes a regular article called 'A Day in the Life of'. Write an essay suitable for this article. In it describe a day in your own life. Remember to describe what happens in detail. Present it in a lively way.

3   Write a description of an interesting week in your life. Set it out in the form of a personal diary.
Read the following extract from *The Secret Life of Adrian Mole aged 13¾*. This will show you how to do it.

Monday January 5th

The dog hasn't come back yet. It is peaceful without it. My mother rang the police and gave a description of the dog. She made it sound worse than it actually is: straggly hair over its eyes and all that. I really think the police have got better things to do than look for dogs, such as catching murderers. I told my mother this but she still rang them. Serve her right if she was murdered because of the dog.

My father is still lazing about in bed. He is supposed to be ill, but I noticed he is still smoking!

Nigel came round today. He has got a tan from his Christmas holiday. I think Nigel will be ill soon from the shock of the cold in England. I think Nigel's parents were wrong to take him abroad.

He hasn't got a single spot yet.

Tuesday January 6th

EPIPHANY. NEW MOON

The dog is in trouble!

It knocked a meter-reader off his bike and messed all the cards up. So now we will all end up in court I expect. A policeman said we must keep the dog under control and asked how long it had been lame. My mother said it wasn't lame, and examined it. There was a tiny model pirate trapped in its left front paw.

The dog was pleased when my mother took the pirate out and it jumped up the policeman's tunic with its muddy paws. My mother fetched a cloth from the kitchen but it had strawberry jam on it where I had wiped the knife, so the tunic was worse than ever. The policeman went then. I'm sure he swore. I could report him for that.

I will look up 'Epiphany' in my new dictionary.

5 Writing about your opinions

Writing to express your opinion is called discussion writing. There are two types of discussion essays. One is when you give the points for and against a subject. The other is when you express your own opinion. First make sure you have gathered enough ideas on the subject. Once you have the ideas, you need to organise them in the best way so that your argument is clear. Express your ideas in a lively and persuasive way.

Gathering ideas

Picture

Look at the pictures and read the extracts carefully.

**'Young people are far too casual in their dress.
This leads to sloppiness in everything.'**

'If it wasn't for fashion, many people would be without a job.'

**'The clothes you wear may allow you to express yourself,
but you end up being the same as everyone else.'**

Question

What do you think about the importance of fashionable clothes
amongst young people today?

Jot down any ideas you have on this subject. Working in pairs,
compare and discuss your lists. Write out in order of importance
a summary of each point you have made.

Practice work

Now write a full detailed account of your ideas on the topic of
fashion.

113

Developing an argument – for/against

When you are developing an argument you need to be able to give **both sides of the case**. You can then try to **'balance up' the two sides** and **decide which one you agree with**.

Read the following article and answer the questions.

FOR

Nuala Scarisbrick

Hon National Administrator for the anti-abortion organisation, Life

When parents first discover that their new baby is handicapped, their immediate reactions are, naturally, bewilderment and shock. These emotions can often cause them to turn away from the child they have created – and reject it.

Some doctors are then willing to 'treat' the child so that it dies. This is not 'letting' it die – it is not allowing it to live. It is causing death. In other words, children are deliberately killed because they are handicapped.

Even though they are not fatally handicapped, some children born with spina bifida or Down's syndrome die soon after birth. They die because they are not given milk – and instead are 'fed' a mixture of water and drugs that either sedates them so they don't demand food, or harms their breathing.

Doctors should never directly and deliberately kill any patient. They should never starve a patient to death or administer drugs whose sole purpose is to procure death. What parents of handicapped babies need is help – help in coming to terms with

what has happened and to find out the truth about the handicap. Parents need time – they need compassion too. No one should either ask or expect them to make a life and death decision about their child – least of all in a situation when they are still in a state of shock.

If parents feel they cannot cope with a handicapped child, that child can be adopted or cared for in loving residential centres. Life has members ready to adopt handicapped babies. There's so much goodness and caring in our society. Let's tap this and treat handicapped people of all ages as real human beings. A truly civilised society would be revulsed by the idea of killing off those who don't 'measure up', and revulsed by the idea that doctors have the right to choose who shall live and who shall die.

114

DEBATE

'It is morally wrong for doctors to let handicapped babies die'

AGAINST
Peggy Lejeune

National Administrator for Prospect, an organisation to promote the rights of parents

Life is never black and white. Those who say 'all life is sacred' are disregarding the suffering of many severely handicapped children – and adults.

When you hear a handicapped person saying they wish they hadn't been allowed to survive, you realise the truth of Albert Schweitzer's words: 'Compassion is supreme and more important than the sanctity of life.'

Some of the lives handicapped people lead in institutions are abominable. Even when parents do take on the responsibility of caring for a handicapped child themselves, it will never be able to make a life for itself. I don't say every child born deformed should die – that's totally wrong. But what I do say is that parents and doctors should consider the quality of life a child is going to have before anything else.

And the decision to let a child die should be taken solely by the parents, in consultation with the doctor. The doctor, in turn, should always seek the opinion of his colleagues. But the final word should be with the parents, having been fully informed of the medical facts. The tragedy of the whole situation is that we have the medical technology – with scanners – to detect deformities in a foetus during pregnancy. So a mother can have the choice during her pregnancy of whether she wants the child to live or die. The decision is far easier at this stage than after birth when an emotional bond has formed.

And this is what we should be pressing for – ultrasound scanning of every pregnant woman so that we reduce the number of deformed babies that are actually born.

Those of us who seek to free handicapped people from a life of suffering are often portrayed as heartless. Nothing could be further from the truth.

I simply believe that the quality of life is more important than pure existence.

Questions

FOR

1 What does the quotation ask you to think about?
2 What does Nuala Scarisbrick say causes parents to reject their handicapped child? Give reasons why you agree or disagree.
3 Why do you think she gives details about how handicapped babies are 'treated'?
4 What word does she use to show what actually happens to these children and why does she use it?
5 What does she say should happen to handicapped babies and their parents? Give reasons why you agree or disagree.
6 What does she mean by 'A truly civilised society would be revulsed by the idea of killing off those who don't measure up'?
7 What problems do you think there could be if doctors had the right to choose who should live and who should die?

Questions

AGAINST

1 What does 'compassion' mean?
2 What reason does Peggy Lejeune give in the first paragraph for letting handicapped people die?
3 What other reasons does she give for doing this?
4 Who does she say should make the decision? What problems do you think this could cause?
5 What does she say could be done to prevent the decision having to be made after the baby is born?
6 Explain in your own words what she means by the last paragraph.
7 Do you think she is 'heartless', 'sensible' or 'kind'?

Practice work   Read the following quotations carefully.

'**It is wrong to use animals in experiments.**'

'**Hunting animals for sport is barbaric.**'

'**Young people have no sense of purpose, no respect for authority and very little to offer society.**'

Choose the one you know most about.

Write an essay in which you discuss the case FOR and AGAINST the quotation you have chosen.

Structuring ideas

When planning your essay structure your ideas simply – the points for; the points against; your own views as a conclusion.

Begin by jotting down the major points. Arrange them in order of importance. You could leave the reader with a question or thought.

Read the following article in which the writer expresses her opinions on schooldays.

SCHOOL'S OUT FOR EVER!

As far as Doretta Sarris is concerned, her not-so-happy schooldays can go to blazers . . .

Tell me once again that schooldays were the happiest of my life and I think I'll scream – because whoever coined that immortal phrase obviously hadn't sampled the dubious delights of the schools most of *us* have had to endure.

Remember those school meals, for a start? They were great if you had a digestive system made of steel, but memories of shepherd's pie served with pasta still make me reach for the milk of magnesia.

Maybe it really is a case of mind over matter – after all, a dish like beef stew hardly sets your taste buds tingling, whereas Boeuf en Daube might have put paid to boring packed lunches!

And as for uniforms – well, it wasn't the principle of wearing one that made me hot under the collar. In fact, a nice, inconspicuous navy blazer and skirt would have done fine. But it just so happened that ours was bottle green and canary yellow – not the most subtle of colour combinations.

Passers-by might have enjoyed the sight of a playground resembling the Chelsea Flower Show, but I can't say that I relished the five years I spent looking like a daffodil in full bloom!

And what about the school trips, which always made the traumas of term time bearable? Everyone must have experienced The Trip to Paris, when we learned to widen our French vocabulary, and the hoteliers learned never to allow another British school party to cross their thresholds!

Of course, my days of eating and holidaying were marred by lessons – not that they seriously got in the way of any red-blooded skivers! The prospects of a day at school seemed to prompt some people to suffer a string of 'illnesses', which often lasted until the end of term, yet always managed to disappear in time for Christmas and Easter. And hands up all those who, like me, discovered that sticking your face in front of the heater for a couple of minutes achieved the feverish, flushed look that guaranteed a week off school and lots of sympathy!

Practice work

Write a plan of the article. Look back at the skill in the narrative chapter to remind you how to do this.

Write a title for each paragraph which sums up what it is about. Underneath each title jot down in note form the points being made in the paragraph.

Think of any other points the writer might have made e.g. teachers. Write the point out and underneath jot down the ideas you would use in the paragraph.

Essay work

Using the paragraph plan write an essay entitled **Schooldays**.

Expressing ideas

Express your ideas so your reader is interested. Try using a humorous tone or an angry one. You can use quotations, examples or stories to illustrate a point.

Read the following article on the problems of pets.

Wow, I'm not being catty...

But as Jane Inder discovered, life with two kittens is more than simply amewsing...

Once upon a time, I would have described myself as an animal lover with a particular liking for cats.

There was a time when my day began with a yawn and by drawing the curtains to let in the light. Now there's no need, as the required light comes through the holes instead. Then it's all just a simple matter of removing little Cyril's limpetlike grasp from the remaining tatters.

Every time I go shopping, I suffer the cat-owner's weekly trauma of choosing between the food 8 out of 10 cats prefer, or the price range that 10 out of 10 cat-owners prefer. I wouldn't mind, but when I recently treated them to some scraps from my dinner plate, they left the meat and fought over the runner beans! Coping with the vegetarian cat, you might think, is a pretty easy task, but I *like* to be able to dip into the fruit bowl occasionally without coming up with half-chewed apples and the odd regurgitated grape.

Of course, feeding the cats was only a minor problem compared with their interference with my social life. You see, it just isn't feasible for a cat-owner to be trendy. The sensible cat-owner chooses outfits that match her cats, so that the hairs don't show. Putting things away properly is often the answer, and few cats have yet mastered the art of picking double-locked doors. But don't be surprised if you see him using your cat-proof cupboard as an emery board. Cats are inventive, economical creatures, and they would rather satisfy this little cosmetic need on the odd bit of furniture to save you wasting money on a shop bought scratching post for them.

But, if going out poses difficulties, having friends round can be even harder. Why? Because, incredibly enough, there *are* people around who are less than enamoured of our little furry friends.

Looking on the bright side, though, you can use your cat's less pleasant aspects to get rid of unwelcome guests. Remember the flea epidemic? That's a good topic to bring up whenever the cat so much as scratches his ear, and it's a great way to clear out the diehard stragglers at the end of your party.

Who says dog is man's best friend?

Jane Inder

Questions

1   Make a paragraph plan for this essay. Look back at the narrative chapter to remind you how to do this.
2   What had the writer imagined life with kittens would be like? What was it really like?
3   Pick out examples of humour in each of the paragraphs. Explain how the author makes them amusing.
4   Why do you think the writer uses so many examples of things which the cats have done?
5   What does the writer mean when she says 'Who says dog is man's best friend?'? What does this tell you about her attitude towards the whole experience?

Essay work

Choose one of the following essays. **Use the skills** you have learned in this section to write a persuasive piece of work. Plan your ideas carefully. Think of ways to make your points clear and interesting to the reader.

1   When you are a parent which qualities will you hope to have yourself, and which faults would you hope to avoid?

2   Depending on where you live (city or country), persuade someone from the other environment that yours is the best.

3   Here are some statistics about motorcycling in Britain, and some adverse comments made about it:

— each year there is a 20% increase in accidents involving motorcycles;
— in 1976, in such accidents, 1,000 were killed, 19,000 seriously injured and 68,000 slightly injured;
— 135,000 new motorcyclists go on to the roads each year, without having to take tuition beforehand.

'The motorcycle is an expression of teenage aggressiveness, a disturber of the peace, and a wholly unnecessary killer.'

'The trouble with motorcylists is that they lack, not control over their vehicles, but control over themselves.'

'I think, as in Sweden, the Government should ban all motorcycles with engine capacities over 50cc.'

1   Discuss the present situation relating to the use of motocycles in this country, saying whether you would make any alterations to the law.

2   Describe all the attractions and advantages of motorcycling.

6 Formal writing

Formal writing is writing a report, an account, or a letter. You need to give factual information. The ideas and information must be expressed in a very clear way. Develop the information and organise it sensibly.

Giving the facts

In formal writing you are not just asked to use your imagination but to work with facts. You need to give the facts simply and accurately. Read this extract from an article on Canada written in a magazine.

The Rockies Adventure

Some of Canada's most splendid outdoors are out west in the Rockies – at any time of year. Jasper National Park is one of the country's largest parks, and famous for skiing. You can pick accommodation to suit your budget, in the town of Jasper itself and throughout the park. Campgrounds range from rather primitive ones to those which are fully serviced, or there are chalets, a selection of motels and some very fine luxury resorts.

In summer, fast water canoeing, rafting and kayaking on the Athabasca River, or trail-riding into the mountains are some of the activities. Slightly less strenuous are the boat cruises on Maligne Lake or the signposted walks.

It does not have to be winter if glaciers are your 'thing'. Columbia Icefield is permanently icy and you can snowmobile across it. Jasper is also one of four mountain parks where Parks Canada Interpretive Program operates free summer events like nature lectures during informal campground evenings and conducted study walks.

The adjacent Banff National Park is another great ski area, with excellent facilities at Mount Norquay, Sunshine Village and Lake Louise. In summer, you can go biking, trail-riding, or rafting or canoeing down the Bow River. The Lake Louise Gondola Lift is Canada's longest, and terminates at a spectacular vantage point. The park has over 40 equipped picnic sites, ghost towns, and even its own buffalo paddock, but the two resort bases for shops and accommodation are the towns of Lake Louise and Banff.

Picture

1 What facts are given about where Jasper National Park is?

2 What information does the photograph give which the article cannot?

3 What information is given about the facilities in both Jasper and Banff parks?

Read the following 'Beginners' Guide to Windsurfing'.

Beginners' guide to

Surprisingly, windsurfing is less complicated to learn than sailing. But it's advisable to have lessons first. A windsurfing board costs about £200 second hand, and from £300 upwards new (seek advice from your instructor). It's advisable to wear plimsolls or windsurfing shoes with suction pads, as the board can get very slippery, and a wetsuit (£80 to £90 new) and lifejacket.

WINDSURFING

This is the most difficult part! Find out from which direction the wind is blowing, then put your board in the water so its sharp end points in a line at 90 degrees with the wind direction. Stand on the board with your back to the wind, and lower the sail and mast into the water. Wait for a good breeze, then gradually haul the sail out of the water until it's fluttering at right angles to the board. Grab hold of the bar, swing it and the sail towards you, and off you go. Expect to fall in at first!

Take some lessons at a windsurfing (boardsailing) school. A weekend course, with eight/ten hours' tuition, will give the basic knowledge you need (price about £40 for a residential course and £30 for non-residential, including hire of equipment).

It's considered very bad manners to move across another windsurfer so that you shelter him/her from the wind. The normal highway code of the water is that if you see someone approaching you on a collision course, you steer to the right.

There are two basic types of club – one attached to a yachting club, the other a more informal affair centred round a hut, or in some cases, a beach. Membership fees therefore vary enormously from over £100 a year to a nominal £2 to £3. Joining a club does have its advantages – it provides an opportunity to mix, hire equipment, race and swap notes with other members.

The season runs from March to October. Outside these months, weather conditions are just too unpredictable. Remember to keep a sharp lookout for sudden changes in the weather.

Questions

1 For each paragraph, write a few words which sum up the sort of information given.
2 Look at the information carefully. What do you think are the most important facts for a beginner to know? Give reasons for your choice.

Practice work

1 Write a guide to your town, village or neighbourhood. Give all the facts you think someone coming to live there would need to know. Include pictures or illustrations in your article.

2 Choose a hobby you have or a sport you play and write a beginner's guide to it. Think about all the facts you will need to give. Set it out like the guide to windsurfing. Provide some illustrations.

Expressing ideas

When you are writing a report, article or letter you must express your ideas clearly. Then the facts will be fully understood. Look at the pictures of toolboxes and read the information about each one.

HUNT THE SCREWDRIVER?

Plastic holdall reminiscent of a carpenter's bag. Useful for saws and other long implements but no compartments to separate the smaller items. Has a reinforced base and wraparound handles for extra strength. Heavy duty metal zip. Size (ins): 24 × 6 × 7. Made by Karobes and available at Argos showrooms for £5.99.

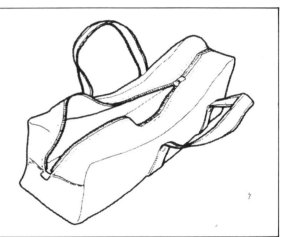

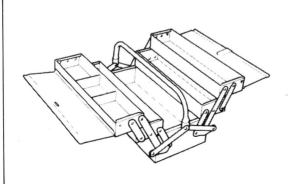

Five tray cantilevered metal box by Talco. One tray has compartments for nails and screws, the edges are turned for safety and there is a fitting for a padlock which will keep the contents secure if not the box. Heavy but strong and well made. Size (ins): 17 × 8 × 8. Argos sell it for £6.99.

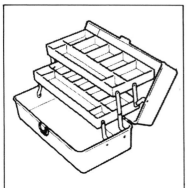

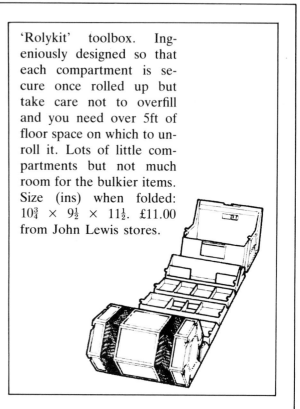

Orange toolbox by Atlas Plastics with two canti-levered trays. The lid folds back level with the base to form an extra tray. Small, light and fine for fishing tackle, or screws and screwdrivers, but not for plumbing gear. Size (ins): $13 \times 6 \times 5\frac{1}{2}$. Available at Woolworths for £2.99.

'Rolykit' toolbox. Ingeniously designed so that each compartment is secure once rolled up but take care not to overfill and you need over 5ft of floor space on which to unroll it. Lots of little compartments but not much room for the bulkier items. Size (ins) when folded: $10\frac{3}{4} \times 9\frac{1}{2} \times 11\frac{1}{2}$. £11.00 from John Lewis stores.

Questions

1 What kind of information are you given about the toolboxes?
2 Explain why each piece of information is important.
3 Read each description carefully. Is there any information you think still needs to be given about the toolboxes for someone buying one?
4 Which toolbox would you choose if you were going to buy one? Give reasons for your choice.

Practice work
Picture

Look at the pictures showing how to do some stretching exercises. Draw the pictures. Underneath each picture give clear instructions how to do the exercise. The first one is done for you.

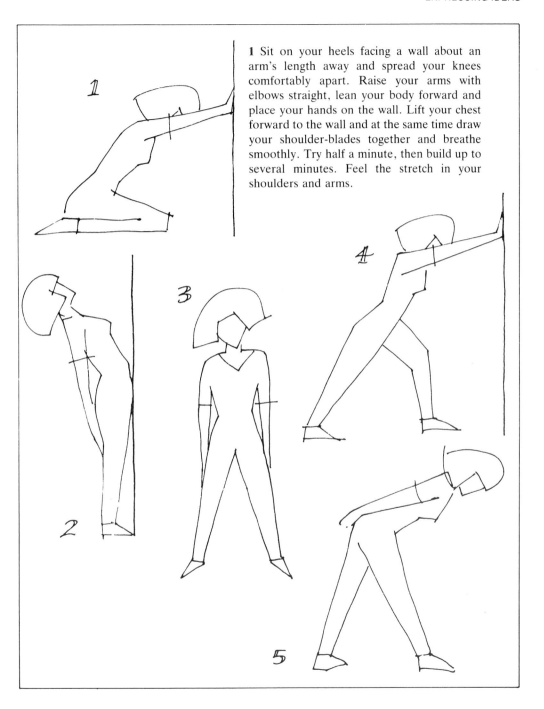

1 Sit on your heels facing a wall about an arm's length away and spread your knees comfortably apart. Raise your arms with elbows straight, lean your body forward and place your hands on the wall. Lift your chest forward to the wall and at the same time draw your shoulder-blades together and breathe smoothly. Try half a minute, then build up to several minutes. Feel the stretch in your shoulders and arms.

Read the information on a child's bicycle.

This is an ideal first bike for a child. It has a sturdy frame to withstand harsh treatment. The paintwork is attractive but non-toxic so the child is in no danger. The fully enclosed chainguard prevents the child catching his or her clothes in the chain. The short reach brake lever allows quick stopping. The soft padded saddle is comfortable. The wide saddle and tyres make the bike steady and safe. The firm stabiliser wheels make it almost impossible to tip over. Both the handlebars and saddle adjust by 4 inches (10 cm) to allow for child growth. The handlebars and pedals have special non-slip grip for added safety. The special carrier allows the child to carry things without upsetting the balance of the bike.

Draw the diagram of the bike. Label the diagram with information you have got from the article. You will need to state clearly which part of the bike is being pointed out. Explain its special quality.

Developing ideas

If you develop information fully, the facts can be clearly and completely understood. Here is some information on how to deal with fireworks safely.

- Fireworks should be kept in a closed box, preferably metal.
- Take them out one at a time and put the top back at once.
- Instructions on each firework should be followed carefully.
- Read instructions by torchlight never by naked flame.
- Extend arm fully before lighting tip of firework fuse.
- Walk away and stand well back.
- Once a firework has been lit never return to it.
- Do not carry fireworks in your pocket.
- Keep pets indoors.
- Never fool with fireworks.

Draw up two columns like those below. Take each rule in turn. In the first column, sum up the rule. In the second column, give as many reasons for it as you can. An example has been done for you.

Rule	Reason
Keep fireworks in closed metal box.	Stops fireworks getting damp and being ruined. Protects them from heat which could set them off. If they do explode the metal box will prevent the fire spreading.

Practice work Write an article called **Safe and Successful Bonfire Night**. In it give instructions on what to do and explanations why. Use the information you have collected in the columns. Add any other ideas of your own.

Look carefully at the following information about how to protect your home from burglary when you are away.

- Leave the key in a safe place.
- Stop the milk.
- Cancel the papers.
- Tell the Post Office to keep your mail.
- Do not draw your blinds or curtains.
- See that all your locks and window fastenings are working well.
- Check the windows and doors are closed.
- Lock all toolsheds and garages.
- Cut the lawns.
- Put valuable items in the bank.
- Lock up your ladders.

Write an article called **Watch Out for the Thief**.

Organising information

You can present information in a number of ways. Choose the one most suitable for the topic you are dealing with. It is important that the facts are organised in a sensible order.

Read the article on *Gregory's Girl*. The information about Dee Hepburn is organised by **explaining the important things** which happened to her at different ages.

Gregory's girl has always been her own woman.

DEE HEPBURN

Age four, Dee made her first stage appearance in a Christmas show at her ballet school.

Age eight, she toured Glasgow with her schoolmates, go-go dancing in old people's homes.

By fourteen, she knew she wanted to be an actress.

So she wrote to Scottish Television and asked for an audition.

By fifteen, they'd chosen her for a star part in 'The Prime of Miss Jean Brodie'. But at school, Dee's housemistress disapproved. "If I tried to discuss careers, I was sent from the room," says Dee. "She simply wouldn't help me."

At sixteen she left school and went to the Channel Islands, working in a travel bureau for six months.

"So many people had discouraged me from acting," she explains.

"But you can't afford to be put off. You've got to go all out and do what you want to do."

So at seventeen she returned to Scotland and, besides theatre work, auditioned for the film 'Gregory's Girl'. She was cast in the starring role of Dorothy.

At eighteen she did more theatre work and filmed the 'Maggie' series with the BBC.

At nineteen, 'Gregory's Girl' was released. Suddenly Dee was a star.

Now at twenty, she's been voted Film Actress of the Year at the Variety Club Awards. "I've reached the level I wanted to reach," she says. "Now the great challenge is staying there."

Building a career can be really hard. And it's hardest when you're just starting.

You need help and advice, someone who'll keep your financial affairs straightened out. That's why NatWest are offering a special service to anyone who's sixteen or over and earning.

It's called the NatWest Young Adults Service and this is what you get.

A cheque book and free current account banking for a year, provided you stay in credit.

Cash after hours with the 24-hour Servicecard, if your wages are paid directly into the bank; when you reach eighteen, you can get a cheque card too.

Foreign currency and NatWest travel cheques free of commission, up to the value of £200 a year, for those under 18.

NatWest will show you lots of easy ways to save that'll really make your money grow.

But best of all, they'll be ready with all the help and advice you need, every inch of the way.

Call in at any branch of the National Westminster Bank, or send off for a free leaflet.

Please send me full details.

Name

Address

NatWest Young Adults Service, FREEPOST, 41 Lothbury, London EC2B 2GL. (No stamp required.)

♪ NatWest
Young Adults Service

135

DEE HEPBURN

Age four, Dee made her first stage appearance in a Christmas show at her ballet school.

Age eight, she toured Glasgow with her schoolmates, go-go dancing in old people's homes.

By fourteen, she knew she wanted to be an actress. So she wrote to Scottish Television and asked for an audition.

By fifteen, they'd chosen her for a star part in 'The Prime of Miss Jean Brodie'. But at school, Dee's housemistress disapproved

'If I tried to discuss careers, I was sent from the room,' says Dee. 'She simply wouldn't help me'.

At sixteen she left school and went to the Channel Islands, working in a travel bureau for six months.

'So many people had discouraged me from acting,' she explains.

'But you can't afford to be put off. You've got to go all out and do what you want to do.'

So at seventeen she returned to Scotland and, besides theatre work, auditioned for the film

'Gregory's Girl'. She was cast in the starring role of Dorothy.

At eighteen she did more theatre work and filmed the 'Maggie' series with the BBC.

At nineteen, 'Gregory's Girl' was released. Suddenly Dee was a star.

Now at twenty, she's been voted Film Actress of the Year at the Variety Club Awards. 'I've reached the level I wanted to reach,' she says. 'Now the great challenge is staying there.'

Questions

1 Briefly explain what were the important stages in Dee's life.
2 Why is this the best way of presenting the information in this particular article?
3 What interest do the pictures add to the article?

TOM FOR TOP

TOM REYNOLDS

First held a tennis racket when a toddler - used it like a cricket bat! Determined to win at early age (Father said) Born — Manchester 12 November 1964

Grandfather — county tennis player - gave support and encouragement. Took Tom to first match. Aged seven.

Loxley Infants and Junior School - no facilities for tennis - but interested P.E teacher.

aged 12 - school tennis team - last! Won first tournament juniors — Highfield District Tournament aged 14. Played first Junior Wimbledon. Not a success!

Aged 15 - joined Bromwich Lawn Tennis Club - coached by Harry Jervis, assistant coach to England Junior Team. 'Lucky break'. Reached quarter finals of Junior Wimbledon

1980 Local schools trip to USA to play tennis. Tom picked. Great experience, learned much. Won Junior Wimbledon Championships as a result. 'New name to look for!'

'A' levels!!! 'Very important to have a career as well as playing tennis'. Worked hard. Good results. Amazingly, reached last 16 at Wimbledon! Aged 18!!

1983 - Good year. Training hard. Wimbledon Final ?? New Bjorn Borg ???

'I'll never let money and success go to my head. I only want to play tennis'

'I never plan that far ahead. I'll wait and see!'

Practice work

Here is a page from a reporter's note pad. It contains notes made during an interview with a famous tennis star. Read them carefully. Write them up as an article describing the important stages in the person's life. Your article must be well-written in sentences and paragraphs.

Here are the rules telling you how to behave on a camp site. The information is **organised in numbered points**. Read them carefully.

HIGH TREES CAMP SITE RULES

1   On arrival, campers must sign in at the Reception. It is strictly forbidden to move in before receiving official consent and completing the necessary formalities.

2   Pitches are clearly marked out and numbered. It is forbidden to change these without first asking at the office.

3   Campers are asked to inform the Camp Office 24 hours before their departure. A day's stay is charged from midday to midday the following day.

4   Campers are asked to keep their sites clean and tidy. Rubbish bins are provided throughout the camp.

5   Do not leave your car engine running; the exhaust fumes are most unpleasant.

6   Dogs must be kept on a lead and must not be left alone in a tent while their owners are away. Dogs must be exercised outside the Camp and not allowed to foul the campsite.

7   An entertainments centre and games room are open from 09h 00 to 22h 00 (opposite the shopping centre). Please do not make a noise on leaving this area.

8 Silence must be observed from 22h 00 to 08h 00.

Cars must not be driven within the Camp between 22h 00 and 08h 00. Please leave your car in the layby outside the gates as these will be locked. Only the sidegates for pedestrians will be left open. Emergency (sickness etc. . . .) ring the nightbell outside the Office.

9 Treat this magnificent stretch of woodland (25.00 acres) with respect. Do not throw away your cigarette ends carelessly; do not light fires. Teach your children to respect trees and shrubs (it takes 50 years to grown a tree to maturity).

10 Speed is strictly limited to 10 mph maximum.

11 Do not tamper with the sea wall and other defences designed to hold back the dunes. Every year these are laboriously repaired by the coastguards, the Forestry Commission and ourselves. To reach the sea, do not cross the dunes but keep to the paths and roadways to the beach.

12 Parents must check that their children do not play in the toilet blocks, nor dig holes in the tent sites or roadways. There are miles of fine sand for them on the beach.

Questions

1 Write down the numbers one to twelve. Opposite each number write one word which sums up what the rule is about.

2 Explain what rules 1 to 3; 4 to 8; 9 to 12 have in common?

3 Why is it useful to present the information in this way?

Practice work

Imagine that you are setting up a youth club in your area. Decide what facilities you will have. Then draw up a list of numbered rules to tell people how to behave in the club. Include some drawings, signs or pictures to illustrate the rules.

Here is some advice on how to make yourself fit in five weeks. You are given information on what to do week by week.

Build-up

Week 1 – Somehow do at least half-an-hour's brisk walking a day. Walk at every opportunity. Use the stairs. Get off the bus a stop or two earlier. Walk to the shops. Spend the whole of your 'jogging' sessions walking briskly.

Week 2 – Start by walking for five minutes. Then jog for 30 seconds, walk for 30 seconds, repeat 10 times. Then jog for 45 seconds, walk for 45 seconds, repeat three times. Walk five minutes.

Week 3 – Warm-up walk five minutes. Jog one minute, walk one minute, then repeat five times. Walk five minutes.

Week 4 – Warm-up walk two minutes. Jog two minutes, walk one minute, repeat five times. Walk two minutes.

Week 5 and thereafter – Warm-up walk one minute. Jog for three minutes, walk one minute, then repeat five times. Over the next few weeks, increase the time spent jogging and cut down the number of walking breaks until you are eventually jogging the whole 20 minutes.

Questions

1 What particular advice are you given for each week?
2 How does this change from week 1 to week 5?
3 Why is this sort of information best arranged as it is.

Practice work

Choose one of the following. Write a day-by-day or week-by-week programme.
Preparing for an examination
Preparing for a holiday
Getting ready for a sporting event
Going through a beauty routine

Writing a letter

A letter is another way of organising or presenting material. There are certain rules about layout which you must learn. When you are writing a formal letter, remember to express yourself clearly. Develop the points you need to make fully.

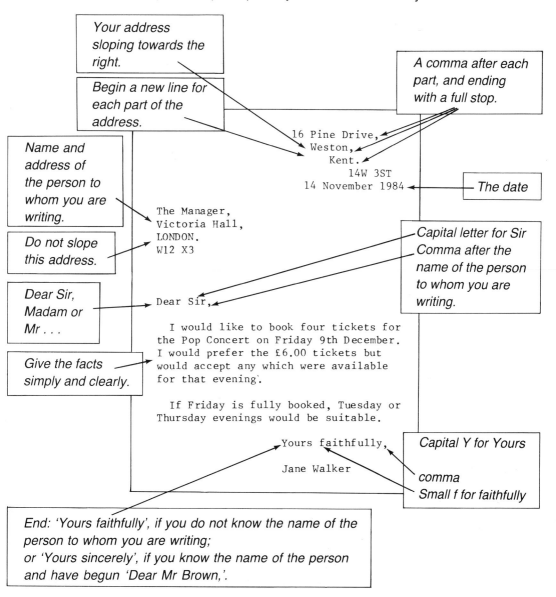

Your address sloping towards the right.

Begin a new line for each part of the address.

A comma after each part, and ending with a full stop.

Name and address of the person to whom you are writing.

Do not slope this address.

Dear Sir, Madam or Mr . . .

Give the facts simply and clearly.

16 Pine Drive,
Weston,
Kent.
14W 3ST
14 November 1984

The date

The Manager,
Victoria Hall,
LONDON.
W12 X3

Capital letter for Sir
Comma after the name of the person to whom you are writing.

Dear Sir,

I would like to book four tickets for the Pop Concert on Friday 9th December. I would prefer the £6.00 tickets but would accept any which were available for that evening.

If Friday is fully booked, Tuesday or Thursday evenings would be suitable.

Yours faithfully,

Jane Walker

Capital Y for Yours

comma
Small f for faithfully

End: 'Yours faithfully', if you do not know the name of the person to whom you are writing;
or 'Yours sincerely', if you know the name of the person and have begun 'Dear Mr Brown,'.

Read the following letters and answer the questions.

```
                                            12 Lavender Walk,
                                               Treetown,
                                                  Shrubshire.

The Manager,
'Odd Crocks',
High Street,
Treetown.


Dear Sir,

      About two weeks ago - or was it three - I was shopping in the High
Street with my sister, Sarah, and her three kids who were visiting me for
the day.  When we passed your shop window I saw this really smashing tea-
set.  Anyway, after we'd walked round the town and had a cup of coffee
in the cafe round the corner I decided that I'd like to buy it.  So we
came back to your shop, and, having looked closer at the tea-set, I simply
had to have it as it really went with my kitchen wallpaper.

      Do you remember us?  My sister's kids were all dressed in red and blue
and I had a yellow coat.  Well, after we'd bought the set and trudged home
on the bus, what a journey it was, I decided to have a nice cup of tea.
When I unpacked the set I discovered some bits of it were cracked.  There
was no way that this could have happened on the bus as I held my box tightly
on my lap all the way.

      Anyway, I'm writing to ask if you could replace the cracked pieces for
me as I couldn't possibly use it as it is.  The teapot's all right though.

      The problem is that I can't come into town for a fortnight as the day
before yesterday I slipped in the bathroom and my ankle's swollen up something
awful.  The doctor says I've not to walk any distance on it for at least a week.

      It would be really kind of you if you could do this for me, and I'll ring
on Friday to see if you can.

      Hope you will oblige.  Thanks in advance for your help.  Speak to you
Friday.

                              Yours gratefully,

                              Connie Chatwell

                              Connie Chatwell
```

Questions

1 What is wrong with the layout of the letter?
2 What information does Connie Chatwell give which is not necessary?
3 What vital information does she leave out?
4 What is wrong with the way in which she expresses her information?

Mr clear
15 Albany Close
Hertford
Herts
2 December 1984

Dear Sir,
  I would like to order two football strips and two pairs of football boots for my lad's christmas.
  I hope they will arrive in time because it wouldn't be worth it if they didn't.
    Yours faithfully
     U N Clear
     U N clear

Questions

1 What is wrong with the layout of this letter?
2 How should Mr Clear have added to the information about the strips and the boots?
3 What is unclear about the way the writer expresses his ideas on the arrival time of the Christmas presents?

Practice work Rewrite Connie Chatwell's and U N Clear's letters as they should have been written. Remember to set out the letters correctly. State your reasons for writing simply. Give all the important facts. Express yourself clearly.

Choose one of the following and write a suitable letter.

1

To the London Academy of Modelling and Grooming at 20 Dering Street, London W1. Because so many of us lack confidence, they've decided to run special courses, called First Impressions, to help school leavers relax at interviews. For information about these one-day courses, contact Katie Hughes on 01–499 4751.

Write for information about the one-day courses. Ask for any details you need. Give information about yourself which you think will be helpful.

2

... the dynamic sound of Dinkie Dean and the Seahorse Angels. This band ingeniously manages to combine the sophistication of synthesisers and orchestral elements of flute and double bass with tribal drumming and the naivety of the nursery, using 'toy computertones'. 'The whole experience should be like watching a film,' says lead singer Dinkie, ex-Slade College art student whose elaborate shows incorporate live visuals in the form of ballerinas, ballroom dancers and demons.
Take our advice and see Dinkie Dean and the Seahorse Angels at London's Embassy Club on 25th November. For ticket enquiries, contact Vivienne Haig, Studio 5, 90 Lots Road, London SW10 (tel: 01–351 5489).

You decide to go to the concert. Write a letter enquiring about tickets.

Essay work

You need to **use the skills** you have learned so far in this section. Give plenty of factual information. Develop the ideas fully. **Remember to plan your essay and make a rough draft first.**

1 **The pains and pleasures of sport** – write an essay describing the joys and sorrows of taking part in sporting activities. Use the following pictures and comments to start you off.

Picture

'It's that magic moment when you know you're the best.'

'It keeps you fit so it must be good for you.'

'It's relaxation – you can forget about work.'

'Sport's not fun, it's more like torture.'

'There's no fun in sport any more – it's too competitive.'

'I hate losing. You feel such a fool.'

Picture

2 **Holidays – rest or hard work?** Write an essay on the two sides to holidaymaking. The following pictures and comments will give you some ideas. Use these and any others you can think of.

'Holidays are for a break, a change, a rest.'

'Picture the perfect scenario: a full moon is shining through swaying palm trees, reflecting the surrounding beach on blue waves, and a tall, dark stranger is gazing into your eyes. Now, what could be nicer than to spend a few, sun-soaked days with the handsome señor at your side?'

'The social life is much better than home – discos, night-clubs etc. It's marvellous.'

'You get a chance to do things you've never done before.'

'Holidays are for enjoying yourself doing things – not sitting on beaches.'

'Sea, sun and sand – that's what I like.'

'Travelling is murder. There are always delays and cancellations. It wears you out.'

Extracts used

147

Index

Acknowledgements

We are grateful to the following for permission to reproduce copyright material:

Edward Arnold (Publishers) Ltd for an extract from 'See How You Go' by P. Francis in *Power Plays*; the author's agents and the author, Michael Baldwin for the story 'Sebastian and Other Voices' from *Love & Marriage* (1946) pub Wheaton-Pergamon Press; the author's agents, Scott Meredith Literary Agency, Inc., 845 Third Avenue, New York, N.Y. 10022 and the author, Frederic Brown for an extract from his *Nightmare in Yellow*; Carlton Publishing Consultants Ltd for the articles 'Now I'm not being catty' by Jane Inder and 'Schools out forever' by Doretta Sarris from *Look Now* (Oct 1982); the author's agents and the Reverend C.P. Gordon Clark for an extract from 'The Old Flame' by Cyril Hare in *Crime Stories No. 7* pub Ward Lock Educ Co Ltd; Constable Publishers for an extract from *This Time Next Week* by Leslie Thomas; Janet Crang for 'The Policeman is Growing Up' by Alan Crang in *The Policeman*; Victor Gollancz Ltd for extracts (one slightly adapted) from *The Friends* by Rosa Guy; William Heinemann Ltd for an adapted extract from *The Silbury Triangle* by David Churchill; the author's agents, Curtis Brown on behalf of the author, James Kirkup for extracts from his *The Only Child* pub Pergamon Press (1970); the editor of Living Magazine for the articles 'It is morally wrong for doctors to let handicapped babies die' by Peggy Lejeune and Nuala Scarisbrick and 'Beginner's Guide to Windsurfing' from *Living Magazine* (Nov and Aug 1982); Gillon Aitken on behalf of the Frank Norman estate for an extract from *Banana Boy*; Oxford University Press for extracts from *The Trouble With Donovan Croft* by Bernard Ashley © Bernard Ashley 1974; Penguin Books Ltd for an extract from *A Question of Courage* by Marjorie Darke (Kestrel Books 1975) Copyright © 1975 by Marjorie Darke; the author, Leo Rosten for the story 'Cemetery Path' by Leonard Q. Ross; Syndication International Ltd for the article 'The Rockies Adventure' from '*19*' (Oct 1982) originally published in Honey Magazine; A. Wheaton & Co Ltd for an extract from *A Lonely Game* by Vernon Scannell.

We are grateful to the following for permission to reproduce photographs:

W J Allen, page 29; Barnaby's Picture Library, pages 125 and 126; Lance Browne, page 13; Central Office of Information, Crown ©, page 39; Trevor Clifford, page 146 (right); Rob Fowler, page 21; Richard and Sally Greenhill, page 65; Brendan Hearne, page 146 (left); Geof Howard, page 92 (below); Tonia May, pages 66 (below) and 92 (top); Press Association, page 145 (left); David Richardson, pages 33, 43, 46, 58, 59, 63, 66 (above) and 87; Sport and General, page 145 (right); *The Times*, page 145 (below); Westminster Bank/J Walter Thompson, page 135.

LONGMAN GROUP UK LIMITED
Longman House
Burnt Mill, Harlow, Essex CM20 2JE, England
and Associated Companies throughout the world.

© Longman Group Limited 1985

First published 1985
Second impression 1987

Set in 10/13 pt Helvetica and 11/13 pt Times Linotron 202

Produced by Longman Group (FE) Ltd
Printed in Hong Kong

ISBN 0-582-22338-5